Richard Deiss

The Palace of a thousand winds and the Gooseberry station

Short stories about
222 plus 2 stations in Germany

Address of the Author:
Machnower Str. 65
D-14165 Berlin
Email: richard.deiss@gmail.com

Comments are welcome and will be considered in the next edition (summer 2021).

Editing of English translation: **Nick Snipes** (Berlin)

Herstellung und Verlag: BoD - Books on Demand, Norderstedt
Zweite Auflage 2020, Originalausgabe
(Second English language edition, original)

Printed in Germany

ISBN   978-3-7519-705-32

Dieses Buch ist meinem Neffen Salvador D. gewidmet.

Bibliografische Information der Deutschen Nationalbibliothek
Die Deutsche Nationalbibliothek verzeichnet diese Publikation in der Deutschen Nationalbibliografie; detaillierte bibliografische Daten sind im Internet über http://dnb.d-nb.de abrufbar

Contents

Foreword   **5**

1. Berlin   **7**

    1.1   Long distance stations   7
    1.2   S-Bahn stations   12

2. Brandenburg   **15**

3. Mecklenburg-Western Pomerania   **19**

4. Saxony-Anhalt   **24**

5. Thuringia   **30**

6. Saxony   **34**

7. Schleswig-Holstein   **40**

8. Hamburg   **45**

9. Bremen   **48**

10. Lower Saxony   **50**

10.1 Hannover and southeast Lower Saxony   50
10.2 Western and northern Lower Saxony   57

11. Northrhine-Westphalia   **64**

    11.1   Rhineland   66
    11.2   Westphalia   84

12. Hesse   **95**

    12.1 South Hesse   95
    12.2 Central Hesse   97
    12.3 Northern Hesse   100

13. Rhineland-Palatinate   **102**

14. Saarland   **106**

15. Baden-Württemberg   **108**

    15.1 Baden   109
    15.2 Württemberg   113

16. Bavaria   **120**

    16.1 Mittelfranken (Middle Franconia)   120
    16.2 Oberfranken (Upper Franconia)   123
    16.3 Unterfranken (Lower Franconia)   126
    16.4 Oberpfalz (Upper Palatinate)   127
    16.5 Oberbayern (Upper Bavaria)   130
    16.6 Niederbayern (Lower Bavaria)   138
    16.7 Schwaben (Swabia)   140

Annex
1. List of station nicknames   144
2. Stations that got an award   145
3. Important railway station architects   146
4. Passengers in German railway stations   147

Literature   148

Websites   150

Foreword

Ich verstehe nur Bahnhof (I understand only train station) was a saying used by war-weary soldiers in World War I with which they wanted to express that they only wanted to go home. Everyone thinks they know what a train station is, but there are internal stipulations. In DB (German Railways) terminology, a station must have at least one switch in order to be considered as such. Everything else is just a stop. The term "train station" means the entire facility, whereas the building with ticket sales is referred to as the station building. The population mostly only calls this station. Additionally, the location of the station building in relation to the tracks allows a terminal station to distinguish from a station with through traffic. At a tower station, the tracks are on two levels (one above the other); at an island station, the building is between the tracks. Originally, the train and traffic vocabulary in Germany was strongly French, since French was an important international and educational language until the 19th century. However, with the emergence of nationalism at the end of the 19th century, German-sounding expressions were sought. A German language association was even formed, which published a Germanization dictionary and developed alternatives for words such as Bahnsteig (railway platform) and Fahrkarte (ticket) for (the pseudo-French) *perron* and *billet*. Switzerland was less affected by this development, where the French variants are still used frequently.

Railway stations were once more important for the economic development of a city than they are today because the railway was the only efficient long-distance method of travel. However, the amount of traffic was far less than today. Monumental train stations such as Lehrter and Anhalter Bahnhof in Berlin had only a few tracks, a low train frequency, and far fewer travelers than today's large stations.

Prior to the war, the Anhalter Bahnhof had about 10,000 travelers a day, whereas German metropolitan train stations today have around 100,000 travelers a day. Because the long-distance transport offer has become significantly denser on the main routes, there is also high-frequency rail transport in large cities. Today there is simply a lot more traveling and commuting than in the past, and although the relative importance of trains due to roads and air traffic has decreased, more trains are being used than ever before.

The Werkbund architect Karl-Ernst Osthaus said, "there was a time when one could speak of station poetry." The fascination of the steam locomotive era, to which many impressive station buildings were oriented, has passed, but the poetry of the train stations can still be deduced in many historical stations.

I hope to entertain with the little stories and anecdotes that have been compiled in this booklet and help to round off existing knowledge about the railway. The book is part of a five-volume series with anecdotes, interesting stories, and facts about a total of 1001 train stations worldwide (titles of the other volumes: see the last page). Compared to the last edition, newly added stations are marked with a diamond ❖.

I would like to thank Hubert Riedle (Bern) and especially Jörg Berkes (Langen) for tips and suggestions for correction and Nick Snipes (Berlin) for editing the English translation of the original German language manuscript.

Berlin, November 2020
Richard Deiss

1. Berlin

1.1 Mainline and regional stations

Berlin's first train station

When the railway was to be introduced in Prussia, the responsible government council tried to warm King Frederick William III up to the project of a railway connection Berlin-Potsdam. They argued, "If your Majesty left Charlottenburg at 8 o'clock, your Majesty would reach Potsdam by 12 o'clock. And now, your Majesty, imagine: If in the future, your Majesty boarded the train at eight o'clock, your Majesty would be in Potsdam by nine o'clock." The king nodded, but asked: "And what am I supposed to do in Potsdam at nine o'clock?" Later his son Frederick William IV said about the railway, "This vehicle that now rolls through the world, no human arm can stop it anymore." In 1838, the first Prussian railway line was opened from Potsdam to Berlin. The terminus in front of the Potsdamer Tor and the excise (customs) wall was Berlin's first railway station. It had one track and a side platform.

Berlin Potsdamer Platz

In 1872, the Potsdam railway station was opened not far from the first Berlin railway station. Soon state guests such as Emperor Franz Josef of Austria-Hungary were received here. From the thirties onwards, electric 'banker trains' travelled from here to the noble districts in the west. During the war, the station was badly damaged and finally demolished in 1958-1960. At that time, the newspaper *Welt der Arbeit* wrote: "The red brick building was not exactly a beautiful architectural monument. Nevertheless, every Berliner feels a sense of melancholy when a stone witness disappears from the face of the earth after being torn down." After the turn of the millennium, the underground station at Potsdamer Platz, which for a long time was only served by S-Bahn trains, finally became a regional transport station again. Across from its entrance is the railway tower of the DB (*Deutsche Bahn*, German Railways) head office.

Anhalter Bahnhof - the gate to the far away distance

The Anhalter Bahnhof, once called *the mother cave of the railway* by Walter Benjamin and popularly known *as the gateway to the distance*, was badly damaged in the war and finally demolished in the 1960s. However, the portal proved to be stubborn and resisted several attempts to demolish it. So finally, the people accepted this and left the remains of the portal as a monument.

The many Lehrter railway stations

In May 2006, Berlin's central railway station (Hauptbahnhof), which bears the additional name Lehrter Bahnhof, was opened. Originally it should have been called Lehrter Bahnhof, then Hauptbahnhof-Lehrter Bahnhof. Yet, the term Hauptbahnhof become more common by the railway company. This is actually not a bad idea at all because many 'Lehrter Bahnhof' stations exist currently or have previously existed. In 1871, the Lehrter Bahnhof was opened on the Spree. It was located a little away from the centre and densely built-up areas but had a grandiose, palatial architecture in the style of Italian High Renaissance. Badly damaged in the Second World War, Lehrter Bahnhof was blown up in 1959. Not far from there, on the S-Bahn (suburban train) line, was Lehrter Stadtbahnhof, which had to make way for the new central station. Finally, there is another station with this name in the town of Lehrte in Lower Saxony. Once a small village, Lehrte became a railway town at the intersection of the railway lines Hannover-Braunschweig and Hildesheim-Celle.

Berlin´s crumbling station

Berlin is the capital of nicknames for buildings. In no other city are there so many popular nicknames. Pregnant Oyster, Golden Else, and Erich's Lamp Shop are examples. However, in relation to the new Berlin Central Station, no nickname has yet become established. In the press, for example, it has been called *Glaspalast mit Wüste* (Glass Palace with Desert) or also *Pannenbahnhof* (or *Bröckelbahnhof*, meaning crumbling station), the latter not without reason.

After many construction delays, the railway decided to shorten the platform roof in order to achieve completion in 2006, the year Berlin would host the World Cup final. A false ceiling was also installed above the tunnel platforms, which affects the planned spatial effect. These changes led to a legal dispute between Deutsche Bahn and the architect Meinhard von Gerkan. Even during the opening, some things went wrong: the station did not react to the opening button, and the inauguration party in May 2006 was marred by a knife attack. In January 2007, on the other hand, two steel beams crashed after hurricane Kyrill. Since then, the railway company has been planning to close the station during strong winds. The station also has an underground station, but so far only a short section of the corresponding underground line has been opened.

In May 2007, the then railway boss Mehdorn had to reap another mockery, this time for his taste in art. A metal horse sculpture, *Rolling Horse* (now given nicknames like Mehdorn's horse), was unveiled at the station, and critics soon found out that this horse was essentially a replica of a horse sculpture (*S-printing horse*) by the same artist Goertz, which sat opposite Heidelberg Central Station. Mehdorn had commissioned this when he was still head of the Heidelberger Druckmaschinen (Printing Press) company.

Berlin Hbf

Berlin-Ostbahnhof and the station mission

The Berlin Ostbahnhof has already had many names. In 1842, it was opened as Frankfurt station; at that time, it was still a terminus station. Later, it was also called Lower Silesian-railway station, and finally, Silesian railway station. After World War II, after the recognition of the Oder-Neisse border by the GDR, this name was no longer appropriate, and it was simply called Ostbahnhof (East train station). For the

750th anniversary celebration of Berlin in 1987, it was rebuilt in a prestigious manner and renamed to Hauptbahnhof. In 1998, it became Ostbahnhof again, because a new central station was planned in a different location using the so-called Pilz (mushroom) concept. One thing, however, lasted longer than the station name: Germany's first station mission (Bahnhofsmission), a social facility for the care of travellers and a contact point for travellers with all kinds of problems, was founded in 1907 in Berlin's Ostbahnhof, and it still exists today.

Berlin Zoological Garden

Berlin's Bahnhof Zoo was upgraded during the division of the city into a long-distance station, a function it lost again, however, with the opening of the new central station in May 2006. In the 1970s, the station, or rather the north entrance, was also a meeting place for the Berlin drug scene. In 1978, it achieved literary fame - it appeared in the title of Christiane F(elscherinow)'s autobiographical book *Wir Kinder vom Bahnhof Zoo* (*We the Children of Zoo Station*). The north entrance and other dirty corners gave the station the nickname "Urological Garden."

The hotel station Estrel

With 1125 rooms, Estrel in Berlin-Neukölln is the largest hotel in Germany. Surprisingly, it does not belong to a chain. Instead, it was opened by the building contractor and namesake Ekkehard Streletzki in 1994. The Sonnenallee S-Bahn station is only a two minutes-walk from the hotel. However, you can reach the hotel even more directly by train. Special trains stop at the hotel's own Estrel station, and from here, they go on excursions to the surrounding area. However, this station is, from a railway point of view, only circumstantially reachable through hairpin bends. The hotel also has its own landing stage for boats.

1.2 Berlin S-Bahn stations

Ostkreuz-Rostkreuz

Berlin's important Ostkreuz (East cross) S-Bahn junction was long considered so structurally dilapidated that the Berliners called it Rostkreuz (rust-cross) and thought it was only held together by rust and advertising posters. Escalators and elevators were long sought in vain here. A renovation had been planned for a long time but was repeatedly postponed. In the meantime, however, renovation work has begun and is to be completed by 2020. However, railway connoisseurs looked forward to the refurbishment with mixed feelings since Ostkreuz was the last Berlin S-Bahn station until 2008, where the direction indicators and station signs were from GDR times, and the station was also adorned with old cast-iron columns and lamps.

Siemensstadt Fürstenbrunn

In the 1920s, Siemens had large plants in Fürstenbrunn, then still a western suburb of Berlin. In order to improve the plant's transport connections, Siemens had a disused railway line of the Lehrter Eisenbahn reactivated. The station at the plant was called Fürstenbrunn until 1925. However, Fürstenbrunn was also the name of a well-known mineral spring, and the corresponding mineral water was exported as far as the USA. When faced with the extensive factory at the Fürstenbrunn station, an American tourist is said to have exclaimed, "I didn't know that the seltzer factory was so big." According to Karl H.P. Bienek (see his website "die Siemensstadt"), the renaming to "Siemensstadt-Fürstenbrunn" is said to have been initiated after that.

Storkower Straße - the long misery (langes Elend)

Berlin's central cattle and slaughterhouse was once located at the Storkower Strasse S-Bahn station in Berlin-Lichtenberg. A 420 m long pedestrian bridge was built in 1937 to cross the area. In 1976-77, it was extended to 505 m to the S-Bahn station Storkower Straße and was thus Europe's longest pedestrian bridge. Its nicknames, of which Langes Elend (Long Misery), Angströhre (Tube of Fear), Rue de Galopp (Galop Road), however, show that this was not a pleasant crossing. In 2002, a 300 m long middle section was demolished, but also a 45 m long section was renovated to become the S-Bahn station. In 2006, a remaining section on Eldaer Straße also fell victim to the wrecking ball. Today you can reach the S-Bahn station and the other side of the tracks over the rest of the bridge, but you cannot cross the closed down cattle market anymore. The former Langer Jammer/ling misery now ends abruptly.

S-Bahnhof Storkower Straße: verkürzter Überweg

Wollankstraße and the escape tunnel

When the Berlin Wall still existed, the Wollankstraße S-Bahn station was a special feature. It was located in the eastern part of the city (in Pankow) but was part of the West Berlin S-Bahn network. While it had an exit (which was on the borderline) to the western part of the city, there was no access from the east. The Wall ran directly east of the station. From the station, after the demolition of residential buildings, one could see the death strip.

Surprisingly, in 1962, the platform surface lowered. Following this, the GDR border guards discovered an escape tunnel that had been dug from the west through the S-Bahn viaduct.

In GDR times, the S-Bahn in East Berlin had a striking red colour scheme with brown window bands. Erich Honecker, General Secretary of the East German Socialist Party, is said to have been so taken with this colour scheme on a visit to a trade fair that he ordered it for the entire S-Bahn fleet. Later this colour helped the S-Bahn cars to get the nickname "Coladose" (Coke can), which was probably not appreciated by the socialist government.

S-Bahn station Savignyplatz and the bookshop

One of the most beautiful German bookstores, Bücherbogen is located under the railway viaduct at Savignyplatz S-Bahn station in Charlottenburg. As you browse through these vaults, you can hear the thunder of the trains above you.

Berlin Lichterfelde East and the first electric train

In the pedestrian tunnel of the Lichterfelde Ost S-Bahn and regional train station, an information board indicates that the world's first electric train, a tram built by Siemens, departed from here in May 1881. It ran the route from the station to the Lichterfelde Cadet School.

2. Brandenburg

Königs Wusterhausen and Amanullah

Amanullah Khan (1892-1960) was Emir from 1919-1926 and King of Afghanistan from 1926-1929. In the course of his modernization efforts, he maintained particularly good relations with Germany. In the summer of 1928, a trip to Europe also took him to Berlin. There, he was given the opportunity to drive an A2 type underground train—which was modern at the time - himself. This type of design was nicknamed the Amanullah train.

The king also visited the surrounding area of Berlin, for example, a radio station in Nauen. In Königs Wusterhausen (König is king in German), however, the street sweeper Erich Lange stood for hours in his oak-leaved gala uniform at the station in vain. Colleagues had allowed themselves a joke and made him believe that King Amanullah would arrive here at the station. Erich Lange got the nickname Amanullah through this prank.

Cottbus' "Bayerischer Bahnhof"

The railway station of Cottbus (unofficially, but not officially called Central Train Station) was nicknamed "Bayerischer Bahnhof" (Bavarian railway station) in GDR times because of the blue and white façade design at that time. Curiously, the station also has a platform that is not accessible via the central platform tunnel.

Dannenwalde and the barefoot path

The village of Dannenwalde in the district of Prignitz fought for a long time to preserve its railway station. In 1997, an association was founded to make the station more attractive. Finally, a barefoot path was laid out at the station in summer 2007, the first one with a rail connection.

Eberswalde and the "Spritzkuchen"

Eberswalde, located on the railway line from Berlin to the Baltic port of Szczecin, which was important in the 19th century (from where goods were transported via the Oder River to Silesia), was connected to the rail network as early as 1842. Ten years earlier, the Berlin confectioner Gustav Luis Zietemann had settled in the town. Zietemann surprised the people of Eberswalde with his invention, the original Eberswalde Spritzkuchen (a special ring-shaped pastry). When the railway connection came, Zietemann had the Spritzkuchen delivered to the station, and soon the town was on the topic of conversation among travelers because of its pastry. Today, a bronze statue of a "Spritzkuchen Youngster" in the station building reminds us of the times when local pastries were brought to the travellers at the platform.

Stahnsdorf - the vanished station

Today there is hardly any trace left of one of the strangest stations in Germany. Around 1900, Charlottenburg and Schöneberg, at that time still suburbs of Berlin, suffered from a lack of cemetery places. Finally, the Prussian province of Brandenburg provided space for a central cemetery near today's Stahnsdorf, which was to become the second-largest burial place in Germany. In order to bring mourners to the cemetery, a separate railway line was built from the connection point station (Berlin-)Wannsee to Stahnsdorf, which was opened in June 1913. The cemetery even got its own station building. At Halensee station in Berlin, the corpses were collected and loaded into covered wagons. From there, they were taken by regular freight trains to Wannsee, from where a corpse transport train ran daily to Stahnsdorf. With the building of the Wall in 1961, the train service ended, and in 1976, the reception building was demolished.

Wünsdorf - the Russian railway station

At the time of the German division, the station Wünsdorf was one of the four special stations of the Allies. It functioned as a railway station for the Soviet troops, as Wünsdorf was the headquarters of the Western Group of the Soviet Armed Forces with 20,000 soldiers. The train station signs of Wünsdorf, therefore, also showed Cyrillic letters, and the population also called the station Russian station. On 11th June 1994, the farewell celebrations of the Soviet troops took place in Wünsdorf, and in the meantime, a book village has taken up residence in the former military area.

Luckenwalde and the library

When Luckenwalde was looking for larger rooms for the city library, the idea emerged to move the library with its more than 40,000 media into the empty railway station building. The station building was rebuilt accordingly, a modern accent was set with a gold-coloured extension, and access to the tracks was created separately from the building. The station building was thus saved from decay, and the station district was upgraded. With bus and train connections, the library was also optimally connected to local public transport. The concept was so convincing that the library was awarded the German Urban Development Prize in 2010.

Calau and the Kalauer

In the town of Calau in Brandenburg, it is assumed that the Kalau joke is a pun from this town. Calau was once spelled with a K and was a stronghold of boot and shoemakers in pre-industrial times. The local shoemakers are said to have been known for their anecdotes and puns, which wandering journeymen brought to the world. The magazine Kladdera-datsch, which has been published since 1848, helped the

Kalauer to become known throughout Germany under the heading 'aus Kalau wird berichtet' (from Kalau it is reported). Today Calau is called 'a healthy little town with a sense of humour' and for a few years now there has even been a 'Witzerundweg' (joke trail). On the road leading to the train station, which at 2.3 km is quite far from the town centre, there is a sign with the following joke: Why is the Calau train station so far from the town? Because the old city fathers wanted it to be built close to the tracks.

Kurt Mühlenhaupt and the station

The painter, sculptor, and writer Kurt Mühlenhaupt (1921-2006) was born on the train from Prague to Berlin. The nearest train station at the time of birth, Klein Ziescht, was entered on the birth certificate. Today, Klein Ziescht is a district of Baruth/Mark (district Teltow-Fläming) and has no railway stations.

Jüterbog and the bear cage

Jüterbog has one of the oldest preserved stations in Brandenburg with its station built in classicist style. Yet, there are few service facilities, and the station is quite far from the city centre. It is closer to the district called Jüterbog II, once a military site with a garrison and artillery shooting schools. But even there, one is not satisfied with the accessibility of the station. For example, there is no elevator at the north exit of the underpass. For decades, there has been an unsightly makeshift solution made of corrugated iron and wood, popularly known as a "bear cage." A bear would actually be more suited to Berlin than to Brandenburg.

3. Mecklenburg-Western Pomerania

Rostock - the Lloyd railway station

The private company Norddeutscher Lloyd set up a direct rail link from Berlin to Copenhagen via Neustrelitz to the north, which also led via Rostock and Warnemünde. In addition to a station building in Warnemünde, a separate station was also built in Rostock in 1886, which was called Lloyd Station. With the nationalisation of the Lloyd railway, this became the main station in 1894. Later it became the Central Station, while the City Station, which was closer to the city centre, only had freight traffic. The main station itself was given a tram underpass with an underground stop for the IGA 2003 horticultural exhibition.

Schwerin main station and the teacher Grunthal

Schwerin's main railway station, built in 1889 in the neo-baroque style according to the Belgian-French model, was not destroyed in the war and has been preserved in its original form. Twelve thousand travellers use the station daily, and when they enter the city, they cross Grunthal Square in front of the station. The square is named after the teacher Marianne Grunthal (1896-1945), who was hanged by SS men on 2 May 1945 in the station square just one hour before American troops marched into the city. SS men had heard Grunthal say, after the news of Hitler's death spread, "Thank God, then the terrible war will finally be over."

On the station square stands the fountain "Rescue from Maritime Distress," built in 1911. The founder, Councillor of Commerce Mühlenbruch, is said to have fainted once because of the revealing representation of Adonis.

Bad Doberan and the Molli

Bad Doberan is the starting point of a 900 mm steam train called "Molli." It was built in 1886 between Bad Doberan and Heiligendamm and extended to Arendsee (today part of Kühlungsborn) in 1910. But why is the railway actually called Molli? The following anecdote explains: more than a hundred years ago, an elderly lady travelled to Bad Doberan with a big pug called Molli. From there, she wanted to take the newly opened steam train to Heiligendamm. Yet, no matter what she tried, her pug just would not go. Then, suddenly he even started to bark. The lady called out after him in North German "Molli bliev stahn" (Molli, don´t move). Yet, it was not the pug that stopped, but the steam train which had just started came to a halt with a squeak. The engine driver had believed that the energetic order was for his train. From then on, the spa train was popularly called "Molli."

Heiligendamm

On his way to Heiligendamm, Molli also stops at a racecourse opened in 1822, the oldest on the European continent. In Heiligendamm, Molli's steam locomotive station has a "Herzoglicher Wartesaal (Duke's waiting area)," where a restaurant and a historical-style ticket office, which still issues nostalgic cardboard tickets, are located. On the upper floor of the station, you can stay in holiday rooms where you will be woken up at seven in the morning by real steam locomotive whistles.

From 6-8 June 2007, however, the station was off-limits to tourists. The G8 summit of the leading industrial nations took place in Heiligendamm at that time, and the place was sealed off from the surrounding area by a 15 km long fence for security reasons. Yet, they had left a hole in the fence for one important feature of the town to enter: the Molli steam train. However, only accredited journalists were allowed to travel by steam train from Bad Doberan to the "restricted area." However, they often did not get the chance to enjoy themselves because demonstrators blocked the tracks. The Bundeswehr, therefore, sometimes had to take the journalists by ship to the conference venue. After all, the Molli summit brought publicity, and with 630,000 people transported, 2007 was a record year for the narrow-gauge railway.

Kühlungsborn

Kühlungsborn emerged in 1938 from three villages, and Molli stops here three times: at Mollis Lo(c)kschuppen (Molli's Engine house), an adventure restaurant in the style of a railway carriage in Kühlungsborn East, and the Molli Museum with museum café in Kühlungsborn West.

Güstrow and the cough drop

In December 1981, German Chancellor Helmut Schmidt paid a three-day visit to the state and party leader Erich Honecker in Güstrow, Mecklenburg, where a tour of the cathedral and Barlach memorial site was scheduled. This time, the intention was to avoid spontaneous and embarrassing expressions of sympathy for Western Germany, such as during Willy Brandt's visit to Erfurt ("Willy, Willy") in 1970. The city's inhabitants were not allowed to leave their homes, and Stasi employees lined the streets. Even at Güstrow station (at that time a long-distance station on the Berlin-Rostock line), from which Schmidt departed on a special train, deserving party members had everything under control. Only a farewell gift was somehow missing. Therefore, Erich Honecker reached into his jacket pocket and found a cough drop. He handed it to the departing Chancellor through the open train window. A much-reproduced image, symbolic of the summit meeting, which was conciliatory but did not lead to substantial results.

The westernmost station of the Transsib

The ferry station Mukran on the island of Rügen is also called the "westernmost station of the Trans-Siberian Railway" because the tracks here are in 1520 mm broad gauge like in the states of the former Soviet Union. From here, there are ferry connections to Klaipeda (Lithuania), Baltijsk (Kaliningrad), and Ust Luga (near St. Petersburg). Important goods handled at the ferry station in recent years were about 60,000 pipes for the Baltic Sea pipeline and the Russian high-speed train Velaro, which has already been put on the Russian broad gauge here.

Stralsund - Art in the station

In 1924, the Berlin painter Erich Kliefert moved to Stralsund with his wife. The Baltic Sea climate seems to have done him good, as he was able to celebrate his 100th birthday in June 1993. Kliefert died in Stralsund on 30 January 1994. Yet, passengers arriving at the main station are still reminded of him today because six decades earlier, Kliefert immortalized himself in the station hall with his large-format depictions of Stralsund and Rügen.

Bad Kleinen

In June 1993, Bad Kleinen station made headlines nationwide when GSG-9, the anti-terrorist unit of the Federal Border Guard, attempted to arrest Red Army Fraction members Birgit Hogefeld and Wolfgang Grams. Steinmetz, an undercover agent, had persuaded Hogefeld to travel with him by train from Wismar to Bad Kleinen to meet Grams in the station restaurant. Hogefeld was seized in the station underpass, but Grams managed to escape onto the platform. There, a shooting occurred in which Grams and security guard Newrzella were killed.

Greifswald and the house of waiting lines

The station of the Hanseatic city of Greifswald was completed in 1868. In the following decades, the student saying that you "cry twice in Greifswald" was probably born. According to the saying, the first time you cry is when you arrive at the uninviting train station on a grey, misty autumn day after a trip through the flat Pomeranian province. The second time is when you have to leave the city you have grown fond of in the meantime.

In GDR times, the train station of Greifswald saw increasing passenger traffic. The Baltic Sea tourist traffic was attended by arriving and departing students from the second oldest university in the Baltic Sea region and workers from the Lubmin nuclear power plant.

The ticket hall had not always been able to cope with the onslaught. Therefore, the reception building was nicknamed "Schlangenhaus" (house of waiting lines, at the same time meaning snake house) at times.

The restaurant at Binz station

In the building of the small railway station Binz, which is located at the 750 mm narrow-gauge railway of Rügen, you can find the restaurant Rasender Roland today. It is completely furnished in railway style, with numerous details from the world of the railway. This is also reflected in the menu because all dishes have a railway-related name. Bear's garlic soup is offered under the title "Zurückbleiben bitte!" (Stay back, please!), tomato soup with cream topping as "Schaffnermütze" (Conductor Hat), and tomato mozzarella skewers as "Drehgestell" (Bogie). The last item on the menu, a lemon sorbet, is logically called "tail light."

Unfortunately, the menu does not include an ICE (Intercity-Express Rail).

4. Saxony-Anhalt

Magdeburg and the Uffizi

The building of the Magdeburg Central Station was built in 1872-1882 in the style of a Tuscan palazzo. Although the station was badly damaged in World War II and the western part of the building was not rebuilt, the eastern building facing the city centre still shows the original style. Some Magdeburgers, therefore, say that the main station is modelled on the Uffizi in Florence. However, they look somewhat different, and the "Florence on the Elbe" is still Dresden and not Magdeburg.

Magdeburg-Southeast and the farmer

The building of the Magdeburg Südost station in the Westerhüsen district was opened in 1895 but is now used as a residential building and workshop. By 1839, trains departed at a predecessor station. An old farmer from Westerhüsen came to the station to watch the opening of the line. He stood in the middle of the tracks to watch the train arrive. A railway employee asked him to leave the rail area. To which the farmer replied, "Well, I ought to be allowed to watch it." The official forcibly removed him from the rails just before the train pulled in. The farmer was sentenced to eight days imprisonment or a fine of three thalers (the currency during this period) for his traffic-hazardous behaviour, which he accepted without complaint.

One day, he put on his best suit and told his wife to make a sandwich for him. "Where are you going?" she asked. "To serve my sentence," he said. She replied, "But I've already paid the three thalers." He replied, "What? You threw three thalers out the window! Since I have so much time, I could have easily served my sentence."

Staßfurt - the sunken station

In the middle of the 19th century, the town of Staßfurt, situated between Magdeburg and Halle, played an important role in the development of agriculture and, indirectly, in industrialisation. The first potassium mines were located under the city, and potassium fertilizers provided richer harvests and cheap food for the industrial workers. Staßfurt became the most important potassium mining town in the world. Yet, the city had to pay a high price for it. Due to mining damage, the entire city centre gradually collapsed: 850 houses had to be demolished, and today there is a crater filled by a lake in the city centre. The city also lost the representative station building of the railway station. Today, there is only a disdainful concrete control room left. At times there were even plans to completely abandon the city, which had important industrial enterprises in GDR times, including the RFT radio station. However, Staßfurt is alive.

Pretzsch and Tolstoy's death

The writer Leo Tolstoy (1828-1910) died of pneumonia at a Russian railway station. In spring 2008, a film about the end of Tolstoy's life and titled *The Last Station* was shot. However, the filming location was not Russia, but rather Saxony-Anhalt because of German film funding. The station of the little town Pretzsch had to stand in for the Russian provincial station Astopowo. It was closed for two weeks, Russian timetables were hung up, and the windows of a modern apartment on the first floor of the station were covered by planks. The railway light signals were also hidden behind slats. The lights were the only thing in the station that actually came from Russia because, in GDR times, Soviet technology had been installed here.

Halberstadt and the aluminium cladding

In the Second World War, Halberstadt, the once beautiful half-timbered town in the Harz Mountains, was heavily destroyed, and the railway station was also bombed. In the 60s, the building was clad with aluminium according to the GDR architectural fashion of the time. In preparation for Saxony-Anhalt Day in 1999, the cladding was finally removed, as the station was to shine in its old beauty. However, it was horrifying to see that the building substance was already quite damaged under the shell. A sandblasting cleaning had to be abandoned. When Prime Minister Höppner arrived by train in summer for Saxony-Anhalt Day, it was hoped that the poor condition of the building would attract financial aid. Yet, the Prime Minister had not brought any money with him, and the building was still awaiting its complete renovation. In 2008, however, the renovation finally began, and in August 2010, the attractive brick building finally shone in new splendour.

Wittenberg's green future

In December 2016, Lutherstadt Wittenberg—which is only 25 km from Dessau, and the location of the Federal Environment Agency - was given Germany's second "Green Station" after Kerpen-Horrem in NRW. Geothermal heat pumps and photovoltaics cover the energy demand, and rainwater treatment ensures the water supply. Actually, this fits in well with Lutherstadt because the reformer is said to have once said, "and if I knew that today the world would end, I would still plant an apple tree today."

So Wittenberg got one of the most modern railway stations in the country, and with the "Old Station" from 1841, the city also has one of the oldest preserved station buildings in Germany.

Genthin and the catastrophe

On the station square of the Saxon-Anhalt town of Genthin, there is a monument with a railway wheelset and the inscription "22.12.1939 278 dead." The monument commemorates a train accident in the station, which is considered the worst in German railway history. On the evening of 21 December, a crowded express train (D 10) from Berlin to Cologne left the Potsdam station in Berlin on time at 23:15 but accumulated more and more delays at every further station, as the wartime blackout delayed boarding and exiting. At 23:45, another D-train left Berlin for Neunkirchen an der Saar: the D 180. From Potsdam, this second train was supposed to go through to Magdeburg. Before Genthin, both trains had only block distance. The D 180 passed a block signal showing a stop at the block station before Genthin and thus entered the section of the line already occupied by the D 10. The cause is speculated to be poor visibility and carbon monoxide poisoning of the locomotive crew. At Genthin station, they tried to stop the D 180 with an emergency stop signal. Yet, unfortunate circumstances led to the driver of the preceding D 10 relating to the emergency signal and applying emergency braking at Genthin station. The D 180 thus hit the D 10 standing in the station at 100 km/h, and the wagons slid into each other. The Deutsche Reichsbahn officially counted 186 dead and 106 injured. However, the municipality of Genthin reported 278 dead and 453 injured. Because the press was under state control and not allowed to report in detail on the accident, and since it took place during the Second World War, the German public has less memory of the disaster than many other railway disasters with fewer deaths.

Wernigerode - University with steam locomotive stop

On the Harz narrow-gauge railway line from Wernigerode to Brocken there is a stop called "Hochschule Harz" (formerly "Wernigerode Kirchstraße"). This university is the only one in Germany with its own narrow-gauge station and where steam locomotives stop on schedule.

Hopefully, the students of the university are not inspired by the railway and complete a narrow study.

Halle and the Goetz quote

In October 2004, a monument to the writer and actor Kurt Goetz (1888-1960) was erected behind the new theatre in Halle. It shows Goetz standing on the main station in Halle. There is a similar monument in the station of Halle.

Kurt Goetz was born in Mainz in 1888 as the son of a Swiss merchant. When the father died in 1890, his mother moved to Halle with the two-year-old Kurt, where he stayed until he graduated from school in 1907. After that, a career in theatre took him to various cities in the German-speaking world. In 1939, he went to Hollywood.

In Halle, Goetz's saying "The most beautiful thing about Halle is the central station" is well known. As part of the "Halle Reads" campaign, the quote was corrected on 28 May 2010 in a railway carriage on Platform 1 of the main station. In his novel *Die Memoiren des Peterhans von Binningen* (1960), Goetz had actually written, "The most beautiful thing about Halle is the central station," with the insertion "according to the conviction of well-travelled people, if they are not ashamed to make this old joke."

The complicated railway junction of Halle, with a main station that is an island station between the tracks, has been under reconstruction for several years. In autumn 2017, the station was even completely closed for several days.

Köthen - the first railway junction

Köthen's railway station is regarded as a historically significant testimony to German railway history. When the Magdeburg-Cöthen-Halle-Leipziger Eisenbahngesellschaft (MCHLE, MCHL Railway Company) started operations in June 1840 and the Berlin-Anhaltinische Eisenbahngesellschaft (BAE) in September 1840, Köthen became Germany's first railway junction. The two railway companies built a Berlin and a Magdeburg station in Köthen. While the Berlin railway station was demolished in 1911, the other, now used as a hotel, has been preserved to this day. In 1870/71, MCHLE had a new station building built south of Magdeburg station, while BAE had the Berlin-Halberstadt station built not far from it. These brick buildings also still exist today, but they are no longer in use. After the Prussian railway companies were nationalised in the 1880s, the intention was to replace the scattered railway buildings with a central station. The new, neo-baroque station building, which is still used by the railway today, was not completed until 1920. Thus, over time, an interesting collection of station buildings in various styles was created. And that's not all, as other buildings such as a steam locomotive water tower, a locomotive shed, signal boxes, and a transformer station were also preserved, all of which are now preserved buildings. The railway station was not destroyed during the war, and so Köthen today is one of the best preserved railway junctions in Germany as regards to its historic architecture.

5. Thuringia

Gotha and the Goethe quotation

When the classicistic building of the railway station of Gotha was opened in 1847, Gotha was the capital of Saxony-Gotha. After bomb damage during the war, the station building still exists today as one of the oldest in Central Germany, however, in a reduced and simplified form. In 2007, the station forecourt was converted into a local transport terminal. The terminal roof was given a concrete band with a Goethe quotation: "For one does not travel to see and hear the same thing at every station."

Erfurt and Willy at the window

Erfurt's main station has changed its face considerably in recent years. The main building was refurbished, a row of shops was added, and the island station between the tracks disappeared. From the tracks, the new transparent station concourse makes the white building of the previous station diagonally opposite and the façade of the former Hotel Erfurter Hof visible. Emotionally moving scenes took place here in March 1970. Federal Chancellor Willy Brandt (1912-1992), had travelled by train to Erfurt for the first German-German summit meeting. He held a conference with Willi Stoph, the Chairman of the Council of Ministers of the GDR, in the Erfurter Hof, opposite the main railway station. On the square in front of the hotel, many Erfurters gathered and shouted, "Willy, Willy." According to the official GDR interpretation, it was not clear which Willi was meant. Suddenly, Brandt opened the window of his room no. 222 and showed himself. The media spread the image of a thoughtful chancellor, and it stuck in the memory of many Germans.

The Bahnhofsplatz (station square) was renamed Willy-Brandt-Platz after the reunification. However, the Hotel

Erfurter Hof did not develop so well after the reunification and has been lying idle since 1996 (today the building is a commercial building). However, it was adorned with a poster "Thank you Willy" and a portrait of Brandt in that window that once opened. In 2006, a competition for a monument was announced and won by the Berlin artist David Mannstein. He planned a light installation called "Willy come to the window." However, the city made a change to "Willy Brandt at the window" to make it clearer that the ex-chancellor was meant.

Vieselbach - between the legs

Vieselbach, which is located on the railway line from Leipzig to Erfurt, received its first railway station as early as 1847. At the beginning of the 20th century, the Bavarian composer Max Reger (1873-1916) often came by train through the town situated between Erfurt and Weimar. He passed through often because he was working in Thuringia but had to travel to Leipzig every week for a course. When he once sat in the train from Leipzig to Erfurt, according to Bernhard Hecker's book *Weimarer Anekdoten*, the following story resulted:

In Weimar, a lady got into the compartment and fell exhausted into her seat. When she regained consciousness, she finally recognized the composer and complained about her suffering: "It is terrible. I'm a singer and have so much to do that I don't know what else to do. With one leg, I stand in Weimar and with the other on stage in Erfurt." Reger, known for his drastic Bavarian wit, murmured: "It's a pity that I am not stationmaster in Vieselbach."

Today, Vieselbach (2200 inhabitants) is a district of Erfurt. The old station building was demolished in 2011 as part of the expansion of the railway line.

Weimar station

Großburschlas inaccessible station

The village of Großburschla is located in a corner of
Thuringia that extends into Hesse. During the division of
Germany, it was surrounded on almost all sides by the wall.
The railway station of Großburschla was also located on the
boundary of Altenburschla and thus in the west and could,
therefore, not be used by the inhabitants. Today, Großburschla belongs to the town of Treffurt, and no trains have
stopped at the station for a long time.

Mühlhausen's `Ammerscher Bahnhof´

In Mühlhausen, there is a hotel called Ammerscher Bahnhof.
Hotel guests have often searched behind the hotel building
for tracks or other station signs. The building has been an inn
since 1794. It is located on the Ammerstraße and was a base
for travelling merchants. Thus, when a real railway station
was built on the other side of the city, the nickname
"Ammerscher Bahnhof" soon emerged. In the restaurant, you
can even buy a "ticket" (one beer and one schnapps). In
August 2003, Ammern near Mühlhausen got a real DB stop
and so to say a real railway station.

Lichtenhain and the mountain railway

The 4 km long Oberweißbacher Bergbahn in Thuringia, opened in 1923, is an interesting combination of a flat railway with a funicular. The latter uses, operationally also rather seldom, a touch-down car (today in the form of a former sidecar of a former small railway). Surprisingly, this mountain railway (as the only funicular) belongs to the DB. The most interesting station of the mountain railway is Lichtenhain, with its open station hall in half-timbered style.

Apolda and the star

In September 1884, the railway station of Apolda was destroyed by a big fire. On 1 April 1890, a new neo-renaissance station was opened. When painting the building, no April fool's joke, Freemason symbols were used. A Star of David can also be seen, although it does not belong to the traditional symbolism of lodges. What this Star of David is all about has not been clarified to this day.

Kölleda

Kölleda is considered a mint town. When the Straußfurt-Kölleda-Großheringen line was opened on 14 August 1874, the people of Kölleda insisted on decorating the local railway station and the first locomotive with peppermint garlands. "Look! Here comes our peppermint train," exclaimed one mocker. Even today, the railway is still called the Peppermint Railway.

6. Saxony

Leipzig Bayerischer Bahnhof

The Bayerische Bahnhof in Leipzig was opened in 1844 and is considered to be Germany's oldest terminus station. However, the portico does not bear the inscription Bayerischer Bahnhof, but instead "SAECHS.-BAYERSCHE STAATS-EISENBAHN" (Saxon-Bavarian Railway).

After the discontinuation of the railway operation in 2001, there were no trains in this station until 2013. However, a tunnel leading through the city centre between this terminus and the main station was built, and in December 2013, an underground S-Bahn station went into operation here. At times, the construction site nickname in Leipzig was "Tiefensee-Mausoleum," after the then Mayor/Minister of Transport Wolfgang Tiefensee. In April 2006, the portico had to be pushed aside by 30 meters with the help of special slide bearings. When you sit on an approaching train, it often seems as if the station is moving, not the train. In this case, it was once really a station that was moving from the spot. On October 30, 2009, the station was pushed back to its old place. The construction of the City Tunnel, which was opened in December 2013, became far more expensive than planned. Yet, dating back to its original construction in the 1840s, there were problems with the costs. The shareholders who financed the Bayerischer Bahnhof in the 1840s called it a "temple of wasted money."

Leipzig central station and the demarcation line

Opened in 1915, Leipzig's central station - which replaced six stations scattered throughout the city - was once considered the largest terminus station in Europe with 31 tracks. Five tracks were located on outside platforms and twenty-six in the station concourse. Once, the demarcation line between the territories of the Prussian and Saxon state railways ran through the middle of the station. Tracks 1-13 belonged to the Prussian railway and tracks 14-26 to the Saxonian railway. There were two station halls, two staircases, and two waiting rooms. Until 1934, no Prussian train was allowed to enter the Saxon part and vice versa. In 1997, Leipzig's main station was converted into a "shopping centre with rail connections." In the process, two of the once Saxon tracks became car parking areas. The station now only had 24 tracks, as many as its rival Frankfurt main station. With the city tunnel and the necessary stairs, more tracks were lost (while two more were added underground), so that today there are only 23 tracks left.

☞Not far from Leipzig, there was another Saxon station with a track record: Mügeln station. It was once considered the largest narrow-gauge station in Europe.

Leipzig market and the missing connection

In recent years, major projects in Germany have generally got out of hand in terms of time and cost. The Leipzig City Tunnel was also affected by this phenomenon. Not only was it completed four years later (2013) than originally planned, but the costs almost doubled from the originally estimated 572 million to 960 million. One of the minor anecdotal breakdowns is that the security control center under the Leipzig marketplace initially had no telephone connection. Because of the lack of a postal address, Telekom had initially refused to lay a line. Only a letter to the head of Telekom, Obermann, provided relief. A second breakdown occurred when a tunnel boring machine had no reverse gear and got stuck in the tunnel. It had to be pulled out of the tube with a specially-propelled Russian tanker.

Leipzig Wilhelm-Leuschner-Platz

When the Leipzig City-Tunnel was finally opened on 15 December 2013, there were initially slight delays in operations. The new S-Bahn Central Germany had attracted many onlookers and the train material used (Bombardier Talent 2) was not quite up to the masses of passengers. Because of the characteristically cuddly front and the white-grey paint scheme, the trains were soon nicknamed "Hamsterbacke" (hamster cheeks) by the people of Leipzig. The Wilhelm-Leuschner-Platz station, designed by Swiss architect Max Dudler, impresses with a wall and ceiling façade consisting of 130,000 glass blocks, which are illuminated from behind by around 700 lights. While the cool, minimalist and almost sacral aura of the underground station is impressive, the clumsy design of the above-ground access structure has also provoked critical reactions. It already bears the nickname Klohäuschen (toilet cabin).

America (Amerika) in Saxony

In Saxony, of all places, there is a station called Amerika (America). In 1836, a cotton spinning mill was built not far from the town of Penig. In the beginning, the workers came from the opposite side of the river. However, there was no bridge, so the river had to be crossed over stepping stones. Because the factory was "on the other side of the pond," the name Amerika was adopted. The town later got a railway connection, and the railway station was, therefore, also called America. After the "Wende" (slang for German reunifi-cation), the factory went bankrupt, Amerika was for sale, and the town was incorporated into the Penig in the nineties. After the flood of 2002, the operation on the Mulde Valley Railway was stopped, and today, there are no longer train stops in "Amerika." On one section, however, there is already tourist traffic again, and there are plans to extend this to Penig (just before Amerika).

Train to Kötzschenbroda

When the railway infrastructure was still in ruins shortly after the Second World War, the station in the Radebeul district of Kötzschenbroda (today Radebeul West) was the only one in operation in the greater Dresden area. Rail travellers to Dresden had to take the "train to Kötzschenbroda." In 1946, The Berlin pop singer Bully Buhlan, using the melody of "Chattanooga Choo-Choo," sang, "'Excuse me, sir, is this train to Kötzschenbroda?', 'Yes, yes, he might make it, if there's still enough coal.'"

In 1983, Udo Lindenberg should use the same melody for his "Sonderzug nach Pankow" ("Special Train to Pankow," a district of Berlin).

Dresden - under the rope

Hanoverians meet at the station "under the tail," whereas Dresdeners meet "under the rope." Before the refurbishment, a so-called rope hung from the middle of the central station's reception hall. Today nothing hangs here anymore, but the meeting place is still called that anyway.

In 2002, the Dresden central station, which lies in the valley of the Weißeritz, was flooded by this river. After a renovation completed in 2007, it now bears a roof designed by the British architect Sir Norman Foster, like the Reichstag in Berlin.

Dresden Hbf

Radebeul-West and the cinema

Radebeul is a suburb of Dresden on the Elbe (33,000 inhabitants) and is known, among other things, for the Karl May (1842-1912) museum housed in his former villa. But Since the end of 2006, Radebeul had another special feature: the smallest commercial cinema in the world (nine seats), which was set up in the Radebeul-West station (one of the four train stations in the city).

Zwickau and the model

In Zwickau, there is the so-called Zwickauer Modell: railcars that run on tram lines from the main station to the city centre. Thus, local trains of the Vogtlandbahn travel to the city centre.

According to the local *Free Press* during GDR times (when the newspaper did not yet deserve this name), the station building itself, a massive clinker brick building from the 1930s, helped create a cosmopolitan atmosphere within the city. In the station concourse, two workers' statues welcome the travellers. Maybe the singer Regina Thoss from Zwickau is sometimes among them because she once sang, "If I'm fed up, I'll go back to Zwicke."

Chemnitz' open secret

The platform hall of the Chemnitz station building, which was completed in 1872 and destroyed during the war, was rebuilt in 1975 in a modern style. It was an open secret among the engineers that the Munich train station hall served as their model. Today, a model from the West is again inspiring rail traffic in Chemnitz: the "Karlsruher Model." These are trams on railroad tracks, yet, they materialized here as the "Chemnitz model."

Chemnitz-Glösa - the potato railway station

In 2002, on its 100th birthday, the 24 km long Chemnitz Valley Railway from Chemnitz to Wechselburg was closed down. Since a lot of sand was transported here, the railway line was nicknamed "Sandbahn" (Sand Railway). Glösa, its southernmost station and now a district of Chemnitz, also had a nickname. Since potatoes grown in northern Germany and destined for Chemnitz arrived and were reloaded here in rail freight trains, the Glösa station was also called "Kartoffelbahnhof" (the potato station).

Niederau- one of the oldest

Niederau station was opened in the spring of 1842 and is one of the oldest station buildings in Germany. In the beginning, it also served as a railway station for Meissen, as the "porcelain city" did not receive a direct railway connection until 1860. The station building - which is in keeping with the romantic fashion of the time, but untypical of railway station buildings in Saxony - was built in the Swiss house style. However, after several alterations and renovations, not much of it remains today. The station is still in operation as the oldest in Saxony.

7. Schleswig-Holstein

Flensburg - the first ZOB

Flensburg once had a playful, castle-like terminus station, which was also called the "English Station" because of its architectural style. The architect was the Dane Gottlieb Bindesbøll (1800-1856). When the station was built, Flensburg still belonged to Denmark. In 1927, a new through station was opened at the "north Schleswig railway loop." The old station was replaced by a bus station in 1931, which was the first central bus station in Germany.

A few decades before the station contributed to German language expressions. On 16 April 1897, the head of Flensburg station Peter Lorenzen called out to the travellers to `Bitte von der Bahnsteigkante zurücktreten´ (´please step back from the edge of the platform´). A journalist who happened to be present conveyed these words to the Berlin Reichsbahndirektion and so they became part of the official railway lingo. Petersen even used a second formulation that became part of the official railway administration language: `Den Anordnungen des Bahnpersonals ist Folge zu weisen´ (`The orders of the railway personnel must be obeyed´).

The Kiel Central Station and the Emperor

Kiel's main railway station, opened in 1899, once even had a royal tract with its own platform access and separate rooms for the emperor. On the east side, there was an emperor's portal through which Wilhelm II could go directly to his yacht *Hohenzollern*. After heavy war damages, the station was rebuilt in a simple way. Only the renovation in 1999-2006 brought the imperial portal back to its former glory, and now it again bears the imperial coat of arms.

Eckernförde and the Kiel sprats

Eckernförde only got a railway station in 1881. If this had happened earlier, the Kieler Sprotten (sprats) might have been called Eckernförder Sprotten (sprats) today.

In Eckernför, dor hebbt se't rut, ut Sülver Gold to maken (In Eckernförde, that's where they've found out how to make gold from silver), you can read these dialect words on a building in this town. The silver-coloured sprats get a golden colour from the smoking process. Smoking the sprats has been practised since the beginning of the 19th century. When the railway came to the region, they were taken by horse-drawn carriages to the nearest railway station, which was in Kiel, where they were stamped with a freight stamp of the Kiel railway station. This stamp made them known in other areas as Kieler Sprotten (Kiel sprats).

Lübeck main station and the Shah of Persia

Lübeck Central Station was built in 1908 by the Wuppertal architect Fritz Klingholz, who specialised in railway stations. Klingholz designed the stations of Koblenz, Worms, and Wiesbaden, among others. The station was renovated in 1967 because the Shah of Persia was supposed to arrive here with a special train from Berlin at the end of his trip to Germany. In Berlin, the Shah's visit had triggered protests by opponents of the Shah's regime, which led to the death (committed by a police officer) of the student Benno Ohnesorg. However, the visit to Schleswig-Holstein was considered a peaceful conclusion to the Shah's trip. As in 1967, a further renovation in 1983 did not fundamentally change the ancient appearance. With its old platform bridge, hall roofs, and low-lying platforms, the station still had an authentic old-fashioned atmosphere and had to stand in for other stations, including Berlin's Anhalter Bahnhof and Basel Bahnhof, in films. Finally, the 2003-2007 renovation was intended to give the station a more modern appearance but also supposed to eliminate aesthetically dubious changes from the 1967 reconstruction. Moreover, in 2008 an electrified overhead line finally reached Lübeck, which for a long time was the largest city in Germany not connected to the electrified railway network.

Lübeck-Travemünde and the time

In addition to Lübeck Central Station, the station architect Fritz Klingholz also designed the station building of Travemünde's beach station. Travemünde, today also is known as "Lübeck's most beautiful daughter," was founded in 1187 and was still an independent town when the station was built. The tower of Travemünde's Art Nouveau station shows in huge numbers still visible from beach when the next train to Lübeck leaves. Actually, it should be called the train to Lübeck main station. Because just as the station was completed in 1913, Travemünde was incorporated into Lübeck and thus became part of the neighbouring town itself.

Hollenbeks special overnight accommodation

Some dream of spending the night in a tree house, while others would like to sleep in a railway carriage. On the track of the disused railway station of Hollenbek (near Ratzeburg) you can make both dreams come true at the same time in a tree house in wagon design.

Heringsdorf and the crime scene

On May 2, 1971, Mr. von Stolz, member of the Bundestag (German Parliament), waited in vain for the Nordexpress (Northern Express Train) on the platform of the railway station of the East Holstein community of Heringsdorf. Instead of stopping especially for him, as planned, the train simply roared through. However, this did not happen in reality, but rather on episode 7 "Kressin stops the 'Nordexpress'" of *Tatort* (the longest-running TV drama in Germany). In this episode, the customs investigator Kressin takes the train from Copenhagen to Cologne. By chance, two detectives transfer two criminals to Cologne in the same train. Cronies try to free the criminals on the way by brutally taking out the signal box and train personnel one by one. Even though not everything on screen is 100% correct in terms of railway technology, the episode nevertheless provides an interesting insight into everyday railway operations in the early 1970s.

Großenbrode Kai

Even before the Second World War, there were plans for a rail link between Hamburg and Copenhagen, nicknamed the Vogelfluglinie (Bird Flight Line), whereby the Fehmarn Belt was to be crossed by rail ferry. After the Second World War, this project took on new urgency, as ferry connections via Rostock were now behind the Iron Curtain. However, it the Fehmarn Sound Bridge (also known as the world's largest coat hanger because of its appearance) and the railway line to the new ferry port of Puttgarden did not open until May 1963. In the meantime, a connection to Denmark had to be established with less effort. The Großenbrode Kai ferry terminal was built on the grounds of the former glider air base in Großenbrode, which had a harbour basin and a rail connection. From 1951-1963, there was rail ferry traffic here.

Süderbrarup and the country doctor

Der Landarzt (The Country Doctor) is a ZDF (a German public TV station) series that was produced from 1986 until 2013. The country doctor Dr. Jan Bergmann looks after the inhabitants of the fictional village of Deekelsen. There is also a train station in Deekelsen. As such, the station is located in Süderbrarup, which is marked with the station sign "Deekelsen" for the series.

Westerland (Sylt)

On the island of Sylt, there was until 1970 a 36 km long 1000 mm narrow-gauge railway running from north to south. With the Sylt island railway, you could travel from Samoa to Zanzibar because that was the name of two neighbouring stations. Today, not only these stations but also all other stations of the island railway have disappeared, and a cycle path has been built on the route of the railway. The only remaining station on Sylt is the DB station Westerland. The green figures and lampposts on the station square show that a stiff North Sea wind often blows here. They are, following the wind direction, placed at an angle.

Witzwort

Several railway stations on the Husum Bad St. Peter Ording line are located far from their town centres, for example, in Witzwort (literally *Joke Word* in German), which is really the name of the place. However, no jokes can explain this phenomenon. Back when the line was built, the world was "still in order" on the Eiderstedt peninsula, and the people of Eiderstedt were afraid that the railway would bring "bad people into the village."

8. Hamburg

Hamburg Central Station

Wilhelm II (1859-1941), the last German emperor from 1888-1918, was very interested in architecture and repeatedly interfered in project developments with his own ideas and designs. When a competition was held for the new Hamburg Central Station in 1900, which was won by the Berlin architects Heinrich Reinhardt (1868-1947) and Georg Süßenguth (1862-1947), the emperor rated their design as "simply awful." The station concourse quotes the *Palais des Machines* of the Paris World Exhibition of 1889.

During the Second World War, the station was camouflaged in wood but was nevertheless hit by bombs. Demolition was discussed, but finally, the station building was restored in the old style. In 1991, the northern foyer with many shops was rebuilt. This helped contribute to the station becoming the most frequented in Germany with 350,000 visitors and 200,000 travellers. The fact that it connects two parts of the city also contributes to this, which is why many people simply walk through the station. During the construction work in 1991, however, one connection was cut: the Südstegtunnel, which made it possible to reach every platform directly from the underground station. Many alcoholics and drug addicts had stayed here, which led to its nickname: Drug Tunnel.

Hamburg Altona - Department store on the platform

In 1898, the Altona main station was opened. According to the Greater Hamburg Law, the Prussian Altona became a part of Hamburg in 1938, and the station was renamed Hamburg-Altona. Although the station was damaged during the Second World War, it was rebuilt in the same style in the 1950s. In the seventies, an underground S-Bahn line was built through the city to Hamburg's main station. The old station building was demolished after the construction of the tunnel with the justification that it could not withstand the vibrations caused by the construction. However, the machines of the demolition company could not cope with the stable construction, and the company had to file for bankruptcy. The beautiful historic railway station with its two corner towers was replaced in 1979 by a low building, which was followed by the concrete structure of a Kaufhof branch (a large German retail department store chain). Yet, only 20 years later, Kaufhof gave up the location, and the building stood largely empty. The building was finally renovated in 2005 in order to find tenants at all. This terminus station is also losing its importance in other respects because a bypass line means that regional trains to Kiel and Sylt no longer have to stop here.

Hamburg Dammtor and the Little Red Riding Hood

The Hamburg Dammtor station, opened in 1906, is one of the most beautiful station buildings in Germany with its well-preserved Art Nouveau architecture. It was extensively renovated between 1999 and 2002. In 2006, it was voted 'Large City Station of the Year' by the Alliance for Railways (in previous years Hanover and Mannheim had been awarded this title). According to internal railway criteria, however, the station is not a railway station because a station must have at least one switch/turnout. However, there are no switches in Dammtor, Hamburg.

In September 2004, the station was selected by DB for a trial. The question was whether so-called 'red caps' should be reintroduced. Rotkäppchen (Little Red Riding Hood) is the nickname for the red-capped supervisory staff who used to handle the trains at the train platforms and give the departure signal. Since the mid-1990s, train chiefs had been responsible for handling trains themselves for cost reasons. The aim of the trial was to determine whether delays could be avoided by redcaps. The trial confirmed this, and from 2005 onwards, "Red Riding Hood" was again used at 14 major stations.

By the way, the red caps originated with Max Maria von Weber, a son of the composer Carl Maria von Weber. This is why they are also called "Weber caps." Max Maria von Weber (1822-1891) was a Saxon railway director, an Austrian court councillor, a Prussian ministerial councillor, and a railway engineer. He rendered outstanding services to occupational health and safety on the railways, and as early as 1854, he drew up a study on rail suicide. He was responsible for the red cap, the tachograph, the introduction of speedometers, locomotive cabs, and even the railway barrier.

Hammerbrook urban railway station

After five years of construction, the Hammerbrook S-Bahn station was opened in Hamburg in 1983 (architect: Horst von Bessewitz). The futuristic design caused a sensation. The station, which lies on an elevated section of track, is enclosed by red walls with openings that imitate train windows, creating the profile of a high-speed train. Only slow S-Bahn trains stop here. At least the colour is right today. While Hamburg's suburban trains were painted dark blue and beige in 1983, they are now painted in red, just like the station walls of Hammerbrook.

In 2019, the colour was refreshed, but a DB website on art stations interpreted the new station appearance as a "red ship."

9. Bremen

Bremen Hbf- the camouflaged station

Although the Hanseatic city was badly damaged during the Second World War, the beautiful main station, built in 1889, got off relatively lightly. This is said to be due to a Bremen ruse: the station disappeared under the dummy of a street that did not seem a worthwhile target for the bomber pilots.

The southwest side of the station square got off less lightly, however. When you step out of the beautiful Bremen main station, you have one of the ugliest city views in northern Germany: an elevated street and grey 1960s office buildings.

Bremen main station and the coat of arms

The front of Bremen's central railway station, built between 1885 and 1889, is decorated with two corner towers bearing the coats of arms of the four most important cities that the station directly links. The southwest corner shows the coats of arms of Hanover and Cologne, and the northwest corner combines the coats of arms of the rivals Bremen (a key) and Hamburg (a gate).

Alluding to the coats of arms, the people of Bremen also say, "Hamburg is the gateway to the world, but we have the key to it." If you buy a copy of the weekly magazine *Die Zeit* at the station kiosk, you will find the Bremen key again when you look at the logo. When the magazine *Die Zeit* was founded after the war, the city of Hamburg was asked whether it was allowed to use their coat of arms in the logo. However, Hamburg rejected the private use of the emblem. So the *Zeit* people went to Bremen, and the mayor there, Kaisen, had nothing against the use of the Bremen key, which has adorned the front page of *Die Zeit* ever since.

Bremen St. Magnus

The small station of St. Magnus, on the other hand, was torn down twice by the people of Bremen, although it had an interesting history. In St. Magnus (the Bremen Switzerland), the Bremen merchant Ludwig Knoop (1821-1894), who had come into great wealth through cotton spinning mills in Russia, had an estate converted into a castle. He even had a telegraph station in the castle tower so that he could control his empire. To receive his noble guests, including commanders and captains, he built a small harbour on the river Lesum and extended the railway station of St. Magnus. However, after his death and the Russian Revolution, little remained of the company. The castle fell into disrepair and was finally demolished. Even the railway station disappeared, and the present sober railway station does not bear witness to the illustrious history of the place and its famous inhabitant.

Bremerhaven - emigration station

Bremen was once an important emigration port for Germany and Eastern Europe. At the station, there was once a luggage depot for emigrants. The railway line from Central Germany to Bremen was called Amerikalinie (America Line), and in Bremerhaven, there is a Columbus station with a 'quay of tears' where emigrants were bid farewell.

Bremerhaven main station and the Klimahaus

In 2009, the Klimahaus (Climate House) was opened in Bremerhaven's Museum Harbour. Here, you can take a virtual journey through different climate zones along the 8° longitude. The starting point is a place that should seem familiar to those who reached Bremerhaven by train: the city's main railway station.

10. Lower Saxony

10.1 Southern parts of the Land

Under the tail and above the ghost station

King Ernst-August I (1771-1851) of Hanover was considered a bitter opponent of the railway. He feared democratization of travel and did not want "every cobbler and tailor could travel as fast as he did." In the end, he had to accept the railway after all, and today there is a horseman's statue of the king in front of Hanover's main station, but the horse shows the station its "behind." This statue is a popular meeting place, where the Hanoverians meet "under the tail." Few people know that they also meet above a ghost station.

Under the monument, there is a shopping arcade, and below it, the subway line B with the subway station Hauptbahnhof (the Hannover subway is actually more like a light rail). However, there is an even deeper level. In the 1970s, an additional underground light rail line was planned: line D. In order to be able to implement the line later, some stations were provided with an additional, deeper station level. However, the line was never built, and therefore, there is an even deeper ghost underground station underneath the main station.

The Hannover System

Due to the construction of the railway - which is located close to the city centre - Hannover was divided into two parts. Therefore the tracks of the station were finally laid in an elevated position, avoiding street crossings at ground level. With this innovation, the city caused a sensation as far away as America. The planners there gave it the name "Hannover-System" and imitated it in New York and other cities.

Hannover-Anderten

Anderten-Misburg is a system stop of the S-Bahn Hannover. Yet, tickets are no longer sold in the old station building, built in 1907. In the former travel centre, the music bar Alter Bahnhof (Old Train Station) was established, whose fried potato dishes are considered a hidden gem. Appropriate to the location, one is not spared on railway memorabilia. This is also reflected during live music evenings. During performances, old train rear lights serve as stage lights.

Vienenburg - the first

While Hanover was originally hostile to the railways, the Duchy of Brunswick was one of the railway pioneers in Germany. The Vienenburg railway station, built in 1840 on the Braunschweig-Bad Harzburg line, claims to be the oldest in Germany, according to a sign on the station building. Other candidates for this claim are a building in Wittenberg, built in 1840 and no longer used as a station, and a building in Niederau/Saxony, built in 1842. Vienenburg almost dropped out of the race because, in 1979, the German Federal Railways had the demolition permit in their hands, but did not follow through with the plans due to a lack of funds. Today, there is a railway museum in the station.

Braunschweig and Seebohm´s wagon

Braunschweig once had a terminus station near the city centre (the building is now used by a bank). However, this was unfavourable for long-distance traffic, and therefore, a station capable of through traffic was built outside the city in the sixties. The model for the station building was (as in Bochum) Roma Termini. Yet, the station's square (which follows Le Corbusier's principles of urban planning) does not evoke any kind of "piazza feeling" due to its urban emptiness, A suburban railway on the Karlsruher model is planned to improve access to the city centre, but progress is slow.

By the way, the railway lines run in an elevated position on an embankment to the train station, as in Hanover. This embankment was filled up with rubble from the old town, which was destroyed in the war. Hans-Christian Seebohm, 1949-1966 Federal Minister of Transport and President of the Chamber of Industry and Commerce in Braunschweig, had the honor of breaking ground on the new station. Incidentally, a railway carriage was available for the minister at the Braunschweig station, in which he could load his company car.

Göttingen - the market woman at the station

On the forecourt of Göttingen Central Station, there is a bronze monument to an unusual woman. Charlotte Müller is depicted, who was once considered the oldest street hawker in the world. Müller, né Kreuzberg, was born in 1840 and was sent to the household of a Göttingen professor's family at the age of 15 to be a housemaid. In the 19th century, the University of Göttingen was one of the leading universities in Europe, especially in the natural sciences. Charlotte married in 1862, was now called Böhnig and had 4 children. But in 1893, her husband died of the flu. Charlotte married a second time and had another child but, her second husband Wilhelm Müller died a few years later due to an industrial accident. When collecting her accident pension from the Göttingen railway headquarters, she was met by a traveller who inquired about the next shop. This gave Charlotte Müller the idea of offering travellers fresh fruit and sweets in front of the station, as there was no room for a sales stall in the station itself. From the end of the 19th century onwards, Müller sat at her stall every day in all forms of weather for almost four decades, making it impossible to imagine the city without her. Former students who came to Göttingen after years were astonished to meet the still active "old Müller" who ran her business until her death at the age of 94. At the age of 92, Müller posed as a model for a monument by the American sculptor Hobson-Kraus, who lived in Göttingen at the time. After the reconstruction of the station square, the monument has been back in its original place since 1997.

Göttingen and the monument

In November 2015, another, but more controversial monument was erected at Göttingen station, this time for the Göttingen Seven (seven Göttingen professors who protested against the repeal of the constitution by King Ernst August in 1837 and were therefore dismissed). The pedestal is reminiscent of the Ernst August Memorial in front of Hannover's train station, only there is no equestrian statue on top, but only a bronze plate with the footprint of a horse. Instead of seven, however, the Berlin sculptor Christiane Möbus carved eight names into the granite of the pedestal, including her own. Some found this presumptuous, making eight out of the Göttingen Seven has made the monument even more controversial.

Göttingen and the clumsy physicist

The Austrian physicist Wolfgang Pauli (1900-1958) was regarded as important, but clumsy. During his time as Max Born's assistant in Göttingen (1921/22), experiments led by him often went wrong. In 1923, something went wrong again at the university's physics institute. This time, Pauli was not responsible because he was working in Copenhagen at the time. However, it was discovered that just when the experiment failed, a train travelling to Copenhagen with Pauli on board, stopped at Göttingen station.

Golfsburg

To introduce the new Volkswagen Golf, the city of Wolfsburg renamed itself Golfsburg from August to October 2003. All place-name signs and the letterheads of the city administration were changed for this period (the W was covered by a G). Additionally, on the station sign, the W was replaced by a G. There have even been proposals to rename the Mittelland Canal, which flows behind the station, as the Golfstrom (Gulf stream).

Wolfsburg - the forgotten stop

Consistently the media reported that an ICE locomotive driver had forgot to stop in Wolfsburg. In 2011, it was particularly bad. Three times in a short period, a train passed the city without stopping. It also happened in 2016 and three more times in 2017. The railways do not know why this is the case and have set up a working group to deal with it. There was already the joke that the trains, rather should not stop in Bielefeld, due to the German joke that the city does not exist. Others speculated that this was revenge for the fact that ICE's no longer stopped in the state capital Magdeburg. Maybe the train drivers just wanted to get one thing out of the long-distance commuters Wolfsburg-Berlin.

However, the situation has improved since 2018, training seems to have worked, and no further passages have been reported since then. However, at the beginning of 2019, train drivers from Berlin to the West had to get used to a new situation as trains did not stop in Hanover at times due to construction work.

Bad Harzburg and the ghost train

At 12:01 pm on Monday, 22 April 1991, the train 3125 arrived at Bad Harzburg station without passengers. When the last car, a luggage car, was moved according to plan, the other five cars started moving independently and followed the rails in the direction of Oker. When moving the wagons, railway staff had probably forgotten to brake them. The dispatcher in the signal box wanted to follow the train first, but saw the hopelessness, and therefore, lowered all the barriers along the track and informed his colleagues in Oker station. They attached brake shoes to the track, which finally brought the train to a standstill there. Surprisingly, a (involuntary) passenger got off: a cleaner who had survived the journey unharmed.

The little Nienburg girl

In 1975, the town of Nienburg celebrated its 750 birthday. In search of a symbolic figure for the occasion, one came up with the idea of "the little Nienburg girl." A competition for the best representation was announced, and a bronze figure of a sculptress won. However, as soon as the jurors had decided, the model disappeared and reappeared later in a locker at the Nienburg train station.

Walsrode and the Toucan

The station sign identifies Walsrode as Hermann Löns-Stadt. From 1898-1914, the heathland poet and hunter Löns often stayed in the Westenholzer Bruch, which today belongs to Walsrode. Here, he stayed overnight in a hunting lodge. In Hannover, Löns was considered a dandy because of his white suits. A strange bird also stands in front of the train station of Walsrode. The sculpture of a colourful toucan points to the world's largest bird park.

Kreiensen and the pushbutton plan signal box

Kreiensen station has a lot to offer to railway fans with its imposing island station building, its many tracks, and its lively railway operations (freight and passenger trains). Even before the current station building was completed in 1890, important personalities had already met here. In 1884, Queen Auguste Viktoria Luise dined in the old station building. In 1889, Prince Bismarck met the Russian Tsar Alexander III in the Princely Room of the station. On 26 June 1931, there were no important personalities in the station, but a prominent train stopped there: the Schienen-Zeppelin (Rail Zeppelin), a futuristic high-speed train.

Finally, on 19 November 1956, there was a technical innovation: the world's first push-button gauge signal box.

Bahnhof Kreiensen mit Baustelle

10.2 Lower Saxony - western and northern regions

Hemmoor

The Hemmoor station, which is located on the Lower Elbe railway Cuxhaven-Hamburg-Harburg, was called Basbeck-Ost until 1992. The website www.niederelbebahn.de gives an anecdote from the early days of the station:

In September 1890, the island of Helgoland was handed over from the British to the Germans in exchange for Zanzibar. A festive party was about to return home from Cuxhaven to Berlin by a special train. However, the swing bridge over the river Oste near Hechthausen was defective, and the repair took several hours. The train had to spend one night at Basbeck-Ost station. Food and drink were brought from the village to provide the high lords and ladies with appropriate refreshments. The best skat players of the village were tasked with starting a skat game with the stranded passengers. Only in the early morning could the journey be continued, and despite the friendly hospitality, the snooty Berlin press spoke of the annoying stay in the "Heidedorf (Heath Village)" Basbeck.

The station of tears

The city of Cuxhaven, which celebrated its hundredth birthday in 2007, was part of Hamburg until 1937. Its Amerikahafen (America Harbour) port was even owned by Hamburg until 1993. It was from there that the large passenger ships set sail for America. This was also used by emigrants and was, therefore, also called the "station of tears" due to the departure of loved ones.

Buxtehude - Parking at or in the track

Parking directly on the platform: this is how many car drivers imagine the optimal road connection of a railway station.

In Buxtehude, however, this solution is now viewed with mixed feelings. On September 5, 2008, a 68-year-old man had a sudden seizure while parking, lost control of his vehicle, rolled over the curb onto the platform, and hit the trackbed with the front of his vehicle. Since there were no passengers on the platform at the time and no train was rolling in, the matter ended without further incident. Two weeks later, a car driver confused the accelerator and brake pedal when parking. Her car rolled over the platform and also came to a halt again only with the front end in the trackbed.

After this incident, requests increased for a barrier between the parking lot and the platform.

Holm-Seppensen

On October 1, 1901, the Buchholz-Soltau section of the Lower Saxony Heidebahn was opened. South of Buchholz, the villages Holm and Seppensen were to be connected to the railway line. However, the two villages could not agree on a station location. Therefore, the station was built in the middle between both villages and far away from anything of note. The inhabitants of the widely scattered farmsteads had to cover long distances on foot, by bicycle, or with horse and buggy to get to and from the station. Yet, the station itself was a worthwhile destination, as an anecdote from Dierk Lawrenz's book *The Heath Railway* shows:

The stationmaster was able to work as a hobby landlord because of the low traffic. Besides tickets, Father Wendt sold schnapps and beer. One beer that was quite popular with the local farmers was the "Grog-Special." Some of those who arrived here by train could only stagger home. Once "Kaß Grandpa," a farmer from Seppensen, arrived not quite sober by train from Soltau. Before the arduous journey home, he

58

wanted to fortify himself with a "Grog Special." Unfortunately, in his hurry, he mixed up the glasses and accidentally took a strong gulp from a grog glass in which Father Wendt kept railway paste. He cried out, "Father Wendt, don't make me a grog anymore." These words showed that he was cured from now on.

The railway station inn has long since ceased to exist. Yet, the station is now, somewhat, the centre of the double town (which today belongs to the city of Buchholz). After the station building had been empty for a long time, it was renovated by an association and converted into a cultural station with a library.

Bergen an der Dumme

Not far from Uelzen, in Bergen an der Dumme (Lower Saxony), a village was once separated by the Iron Curtain from its railway station (on the "Amerika" line) in what is now Saxony-Anhalt.

Eschede and the premonition

Situated on the Celle-Hamburg line, Eschede in Lower Saxony was connected to the railway network as early as 1847. However, the small town never had a representative station building. The modest historical station building was demolished in 1977 and replaced by a functional DB type building. Yet, the municipality did not see this building as a suitable entrance for tourists and had the station building bought with the intention of developing it according to their own plans. When the 150th anniversary of the station was celebrated in 1997, the project was promoted with the slogan "Es bahnt sich was an in Eschede (Something is coming to Eschede) " which was written in large letters on the station building. From today's point of view, it was a bad premonition, because only a year later a broken wheel derailed the ICE high speed train in the station, probably the biggest

German railway disaster since the Second World War. A memorial at the station today commemorates the 101 people who died in the accident.

Eschede and Arno Schmidt

At Eschede railway station, two metal plates on the platform in the direction of Hannover show the number 37. The following quotation by the writer Arno Schmidt (1914-1979) can be read on them: 'What does New York mean here? Big city is big city, I have been to Hannover several times'. One thinks of Schmidt's last residential address Bargfeld 37 in Eldingen, not far from Eschede. But 37 seems to stand more for the minute of departure of the trains to Hannover. On the platform for the other direction you will find correspondingly the figure18.

Number 37 at the Eschede station

Uelzen - the Hundertwasser railway station

In 2000, the Austrian painter Friedensreich Hundertwasser died. He was almost more famous for his buildings than his artworks. Even after his death, many buildings designed by him were still left to be realized. For the World Expo 2000, Uelzen in Lower Saxony wanted to shine with a special building project. Therefore, it was decided to redesign the city's sober brick station in the sense of Hundertwasser architecture (like the famous house in Vienna). At the same time, it was decided to make it also an environmental station. Even the toilets are designed in the Hundertwasser style.

Ganderkesee's mysterious station tile

The station of Ganderkesee was destroyed by British tanks at the end of the Second World War. A new building was completed in 1949. An unknown person had put the following local dialect slogan on a brick of the new station, which can still be read today, "Und wen alles vergeit, de Bohnhof steit (And if everything crumbles, the station will not tumble)."

When the station was converted into the restaurant "Gleis Eins" a few years ago, the brick just protruded under a newly moved-in wooden surface. The Heimatverein Ganderkesee, which sees the brick as an important artifact, saw the intactness and visibility of the brick endangered and is trying (so far unsuccessfully) to find out the author of the brick inscription.

Oldenburg's clinker castle

Oldenburg Central Station has a long name because you have to say "Oldenburg in Oldenburg" so that the station is not confused with Oldenburg in Holstein. At one point, a writer is said to have arrived in the wrong Oldenburg. He was surprised that there was no evidence of the inviting literary society to be seen. On the other hand, some people wondered whether the addition of Hauptbahnhof (central station) to the station's name was necessary since there was no other train station in Oldenburg. In timetables, it is only called Oldenburg. However, when the new Oldenburg-Wechloy station was opened in 2015, the additional naming was once again justified.

The Art Nouveau-styled Central Station, built in 1915, used to have another name. It was called "Klinkerburg" (clinker castle) because of its building material and its tower-like appearance. Klinkerburg is also the name of the Art Nouveau restaurant in the station, which is one of the most beautiful station restaurants in Germany. There you can also order the local speciality Grünkohl mit Pinkel (kale with spiced local sausage).

Oldenburg Hbf

Osnabrück old town station

Osnabrück main station is a strange station because two railway lines cross in the station. It has two levels and is, therefore, considered a tower station. When Osnabrück's main railway station was opened in 1895 as a central railway station far from the city centre, businessmen in Hasenstrasse on the edge of the old town feared a drop in sales. They pushed for the establishment of a station in the area, which was realised in 1896. However, more than 600 citizens of the city donated more than the required 40,000 marks for the project. The remaining sum was used to support the construction of the city's theatre at the Domhof. In 1968, the half-timbered station building was demolished and replaced by a functional new concrete building.

Because the building was close to the bishop's seat, the station was soon nicknamed "Catholic station." Visitors to the nearby theatre, some of whom arrived here on special trains, also called it "theatre station." In December 2009, there was an official change of name to the station. To make its location near the old town clearer, the Hasetor stop was renamed Osnabrück Altstadt (Old Town).

Emden and the Marschboden

The main station of Emden is a simple concrete cube with window bands built in the 70s, and even platform underpasses are also missing. The reason: the marsh soil makes civil engineering measures expensive. The platforms are, therefore, reached by overpasses.

The Weserschlösschen

Since Blexen is located at the mouth of the Weser opposite the former emigrant port of Bremerhaven, the present district of Nordenham was once jokingly called "the last village before America." Blexen's train station even reminds one somewhat of America because of its eclectic style with turrets and battlements reminiscent of Disneyland. It was called "Weserschlösschen" (Little Weser Castle) by the population because of its appearance. Today the building houses the Weserschlösschen restaurant, and ferries to Bremerhaven leave from the former railway station.

Bad Bentheim

In 2016, the train station of Bad Bentheim had the most famous train station window in Germany. After the platforms were raised by 40 cm to make it easier for wheelchair users to enter the trains, the station doors to the tracks could no longer be opened. Although it was also possible to walk around the station building, some passengers simply climbed onto the platform out of the window. These scenes could be observed from the long-distance trains Berlin-Amsterdam. The media jumped on this alleged prank, and soon the city was called Bad Doofheim, (Doof meaning daft). Only a few years later, however, there was more positive news. The dilapidated station and ugly duckling had become Bad Schönheim (Schön meaning beautiful) after a completed renovation. The ominous climbing window is now displayed in the entrance area, labelled with quotes from the press. In July 2019, the Bad Bentheim-Nordhorn-Neuenhaus railway, which had long been shut down for passenger traffic, was also put back into operation. In autumn of the same year, Bad Bentheim was also named Station of the Year by the Pro-Rail Alliance.

Leer and the spoons

In the SAT.1 (a German public channel) quiz show "Genial daneben" (Ingeniously wrong), the participants had to guess why the teaspoons in the station café of Leer had holes in them. The solution to the riddle is as follows:
There is also a drug problem in the tranquil East Frisian town of Leer. One of the focal points for the drug scene is the town's train station. Here, junkies used the spoons of the station café to boil heroin with water over a candle for a hit. In the station café at Leer station, teaspoons with holes in the middle that are unsuitable for cooking are, therefore, handed out. In recent years, the drug problem at the station has decreased. However, when you step out of the station

building, which was built in 1856 in a classical architectural language, you are confronted with a nautical sculpture installed on a roundabout, which reminds you of a giant syringe.

Leer Station

11. North Rhine-Westphalia

11.1 NRW-Rhineland

Aachen - the first " Bahnhof"(station)

Since progress in Europe came from the West for a long time, many things in Germany happened first in Aachen. Germany's first hot air balloon rose in Aachen (1786), Aachen was the first German industrial city, and Aachen had the first railway viaduct in Germany. According to Richard Wollgarten in his book *Einzig Aachen* (Aachen 2009), the word Bahnhof (train station in German) came from Aachen. This term for railway station was coined during the construction of the Rheinische Eisenbahn, which began in 1838. When the building materials were stored in Aachen, the word station was used instead of building yard, as was usually the case.

Today the station sign of the station, which was renovated in 2006, should actually say Bad Aachen because the city is a spa and health resort (Bad means bath in German). Yet, Aachen likes to be at the very beginning of the alphabet and, therefore, rarely uses the bath addition.

In 1843, the Aachen-Antwerp line was opened, the first international railway line in the world.

Herzogenrath

The letters E*urode* can be read at Herzogenrath station. This is the name for the symbolic European city of Herzogenrath (DE) and Kerkrade (NL). Rode also stands for the castle Rode, from which the name Herzogenrath is derived, whereas Eur or Eu stands for Europe.

Many Dutch people use Herzogenrath station to travel to Aachen. There are Dutch ticket machines and ticket validators at the station.

Herzogenrath and Moses

Near Herzogenrath, in 1852, a sandstone was discovered which was particularly strong and durable. In order to make it known, a local engineer commissioned the sculptor Wings from Baesweiler to create a large Moses figure from the stone. They were so proud of this 3.5 m high, 7.5 ton figure that it was sent to the World Exhibition in Paris in 1856. However, it did not find a buyer there. So it was sent back to Herzogenrath by train, where it lay around in the station area for a long time. Eventually a use for it was found, it was placed on the station square. The platform made of wooden sleepers rotted over time and finally Moses fell on his nose. After it had been rebult- Moses had also been given a new nose - the people of Herzogenrath celebrated a Moses resurrection festival. Later the station was extended and Moses had to make way and Moses' transfer was celebrated. There, at a place not far from the station, he stood for several decades until times got worse. This Israelite seems to have been a thorn in the side of the Nazis. One night in February 1934, Moses was torn from his pedestal and disappeared.

It was not until 1962, when a local needle manufacturer gave a donation, that a new Moses was installed. When the new monument was unveiled on 8 September 1962, however, the cheers were limited, as the new Moses was much smaller than the previous model. In 1997, the pedestal was broken when the figure was moved again. In 2002 the work of art was finally rededicated with a new basalt pedestal. But this was not the end of the story. In the night from 22nd to 23rd April 2014 the bronze figure was stolen again. When I visited Herzogenrath in October 2020, still only the empty basalt pedestal was visible.

Cologne central station - the station chapel

In 1859, the central railway station, located next to the cathedral, was opened in Cologne. At the same time, a railway bridge over the Rhine was put into operation. The Prussian King Friedrich Wilhelm IV had the bridge axis built exactly into the extension of the longitudinal axis of the cathedral. The cathedral is aligned in a west-east direction (towards Jerusalem), and as in many cathedrals, the towers stand in the west. Even today, the trains running from the Deutz side over the Hohenzollern Bridge to the main station seem to be heading towards the cathedral. When the cathedral bridge was built, however, the view was quite different. The construction of Cologne Cathedral, begun in 1248, was stopped in 1560 without completing the towers. Therefore, the cathedral had blunt towers, like the Notre-Dame church in Paris. In the 19th century, when the Rhineland became part of Prussia, the gothic architecture experienced a new appreciation by king Friedrich Wilhelm IV. In 1880, the spires were completed in their present form. In the shadow of the building, is the main railway station, which is so modestly crouched in front of the cathedral. Therefore, it is also called the "station chapel."

The number 11 is considered a "holy number" by the people of Solothurn. Some wonder whether eleven is also Cologne's (secret) holy number. Cologne's "fifth season" (the carnival) begins on 11.11, the city suffers from the failings of the eleven players of local club FC Köln, the Eau de Cologne-number 4711 contains the eleven, and finally, the main station also has eleven tracks.

Cologne-Deutz and the millionth guest worker

On the morning of 10 September 1964, journalists were stepping on each other's toes at the Cologne-Deutz station. At 10:10, a train with Spanish and Portuguese guest workers arrived. One of them was supposed to be the Portuguese

Armando Rodrigues, whom the Federal Association of German Employers (BDA) had identified as the millionth guest worker in Germany. Since 24 Portuguese had been sent back at the border, it was hoped that Rodrigues was not among the rejected. A first train arrived, but Rodrigues was not among the passengers. A second train arrived, and an interpreter walked along the platform shouting "Armando Rodrigues, Armando Rodrigues." When he had almost run out of passengers to question, a Mr. Rodrigues, who did not know what was happening to him, hesitantly called at the end of the platform. A little later, the Portuguese man, who was somewhat exhausted after 48 hours on the train, was in the spotlight. As the millionth guest worker, he received a moped - which now stands in the Bonn House of History - as a gift.

Cologne Messe (Fair)/Deutz

Starting in 2009, the Köln-Messe/Deutz railway station was renovated for several years. Although the aesthetically pleasing round of the entrance hall soon proved successful, the condition of the intersection station, with its complex routing, was not convincing at first. In December 2009, the Kölner Verkehrsverein awarded the station the "Sour Lemon" for the ugliest place in Cologne. In the years that followed, however, the station was partially refurbished.

On the stairs leading up to the main entrance of the station, there is a monument to Nicolaus Otto and Eugen Langen. Otto inventor of the engine named after him. Langen was the founder of Motorenfabrik Deutz - today's Deutz AG - and father of the Wuppertal (and Dresden) suspension railway.

Cologne Holweide and the memorial railway station

The development of today's S-Bahn station Köln-Holweide is closely linked to football. The former SC Preußen Dellbrück (later to become Viktoria Köln on the right bank of the Rhine) had a venue nearby. Since many fans came from Holweide and wanted to board special soccer trains there, they applied for a stop. The German Federal Railways only wanted to accommodate this request if a ramp was built for getting on and off the train. This was no problem for the chairman of the club Willy Röhrig because he was a building contractor. He had a stop built in a short time without bureaucratic interference. The German Federal Railways recognised this new station, and soon, trains stopped even outside football matches. The locals soon called the station "Willy Röhrig Memorial Station." From 1975, suburban trains of the Chorweiler-Bergisch-Gladbach line stopped here.

Cologne Eifeltor and the removal

On 5 July 1999, the first container train with removal goods from the German government left Cologne-Eifeltor and arrived the next day at Berlin's Hamburger and Lehrter stations. A total of 1216 containers were brought to Berlin in 19 trains. The containers were filled with 37,000 metres of files but also 837 refrigerators and 7,500 bottles of wine.

Bonn main station

Bonn's main station building was built in 1884 in a representative neo-renaissance style. After all, Hohenzollern princes studied in the city. The façade resembles the former Lehrter Bahnhof in Berlin and survived World War II without damage. In 1949, the station experienced a great increase in importance, as Bonn became the seat of the West German government. Politicians and federal officials arrived here by train. However, the station is not particularly large as it only has five tracks. That is why there was the saying: 'Traveler, if you come to Bonn, don't look for the main station - it is it'. However, many trains ran on this important north-south axis. For Bonn the saying applied: 'Either it's raining or the railway barriers are down'. In the station there is an underground light rail stop, which was intended to serve as a protective bunker in case of emergency. Due to the relocation of the government and the new Cologne-Frankfurt line, which passes Bonn, the station lost some of its importance, but also smokers. In 2002, the station became the first non-smoking station of the DB.

Bonn and the "little station"

Opened in 1860 (initially as a horse-drawn railway), the Bröltalbahn was the first public narrow-gauge railway in Germany (gauge 785 mm). It was mainly used for freight traffic. One important good was the rock basalt, which was transferred to ships in Beuel. In today's Bonn district of Beuel, there is also the only preserved station building of the Bröltalbahn, which was discontinued in 1956 for passenger traffic and in 1967 for freight traffic. The now restored station building serves as a restaurant today. Where there were once tracks, one of Bonn's most popular beer gardens can now be found on the banks of the Rhine.

Bonns ‚Bahnhöfchen'

Krefeld and the appropriate opening move

Krefeld's first railway station, built in the 1850s, was soon an obstacle to other traffic with its ground-level tracks. Therefore, the Prussian parliament agreed to a renovation by raising of the tracks on a dam through the city. On 3 December, the main station, which still exists today, was finally opened. The website of the city of Krefeld gives the following anecdote under the topic "When the railway came to Krefeld":

The opening was to take place without a big event. Yet, when the Aachen-Berlin Krefeld express train passed through Krefeld shortly before midnight the day before, the train driver thought that the station should be inaugurated by a proper train. Therefore, he stopped in the new station concourse at 23:52 on 2nd December. However, there was no staff on the tracks, and the passengers getting off soon found themselves in front of locked doors. After wandering through the building, they returned to the train. After all, midnight had passed, and the calendar day of the official inauguration had been reached.

Leverkusen-Mitte - 'the station toilet'

Despite a population of over 160,000 and several train stations, the city of Leverkusen does not have a central station. Until the early 20th century, there was not even the possibility of a railway station called Leverkusen. It was only in 1930 that the city was given the name Leverkusen after several communities were incorporated into the town of Wiesdorf. The city was named after the pharmacist and founder of the chemical works Carl Leverkus (1804-1889). In 1914, Wiesdorf was given a train station. In 1979, the more centrally located Leverkusen Mitte station was opened. However, it was so modest that it is popularly called the "Bahnhofsklo" (station toilet). Nevertheless, it was given a glass gable by the Leverkusen artist Paul Weigmann (1924-

2009), whose stained-glass windows adorn 300 churches in Germany. However, the work of art at the station is not decorated with a church cross but with a Bayer cross, as this pharmaceutical company was a sponsor. However, you have to enter the station building to appreciate the play of colours in the glass windows. Despite the work of art, the station building will be demolished in the next few years because it lies in the path of additional track, which is necessary for the planned Rhein-Ruhr-Express. However, this would also allow Leverkusen to build a more representative railway entrance for an important city in the German Bundesliga (German football league). Perhaps there will then be a toilet in the station because you won't find a station toilet in the "Bahnhofsklo" today.

Leverkusen Mitte

Duisburg Central Station and the Royals

The design of Duisburg's main railway station, completed in 1934, was once regarded as groundbreaking. Through traffic (and formerly also the tram) runs in a trench in front of the station, which was bridged by a cover that allowed pedestrians and feeder traffic to reach the station unhindered. By the way, Duisburg's main station is similar to the former southern and today's main station of Königsberg, which was built in 1929. The protruding front of the clearly structured Duisburg station building, with an inconspicuous station clock hanging in the middle, offers protection from the weather. In the 1960s, the station clock almost caused a catastrophe. When Prince Philip and Queen Elizabeth II of England paid their respects to Duisburg station during a state visit, the master of ceremonies overlooked the low-hanging clock. In the open coupé, the tall prince headed straight for the clock but was able to duck away at the last moment.

Essen - the blue light

With 175,000 passengers a day, Essen's main railway station is one of the largest stations in North Rhine-Westphalia. Yet, architecturally speaking, the post-war building is not exactly a figurehead. Since there was no possibility of expansion, there were plans to move the station to the west. However, after the station in the neighbouring city of Gelsenkirchen was successfully renovated for the World Cup at a reasonable price, the existing building was also renovated in Essen. In January 2010, the renovated station was opened for the Capital of Culture year. The rails of this through station are located at a high level, below which are levels with shops and ticket counters. The station also has an underground tram station bathed in blue light, which is surprisingly another indicator of the station's social standing. For once, the drug scene was forced out of the city into the station. The light is also blue so that junkies do not find their veins when injecting and thus avoid this place.

Essen Hügel

The construction of Essen's Hügel train station is thanks to the steel entrepreneur Friedrich Alfred Krupp (1854-1902). In 1870, the gigantic Villa Krupp was built in the south of Essen. To make it easier for state guests and industrialists to

74

get to the station, Krupp had a railway station built in 1890 on the site of the Hügel park, which belonged to him. This was also intended to serve the general public, as the Ruhr valley - through which the Bergisch-Märkische railway line ran - was a popular local recreation area. Krupp paid for the construction of the station, but the state had to pay for its maintenance. For Friedrich Alfred Krupp himself, there was a special permit to reach Hügel station through a Hügelpark gate. Later, family members and employees of the Krupp company were granted further special permits. Direct access was also granted to state guests. When the King of Egypt paid a visit in June 1929, Krupp issued identity cards to enter the platforms to keep the public entertained. Not everyone liked this. In response, the local press in Essen asked, "Who owns Bahnhof Hügel?" To avoid negative press, such identity cards were later issued by the railway.

Hugo Stinnes and the urge to go to Essen

The German industrialist Hugo Stinnes (1870-1924) built up the largest German corporation after the First World War. In 1924, when Stinnes died, the family owned 3000 enterprises and, with 600,000 employees, was the largest employer in the world. After the death of Hugo Stinnes, however, the company quickly disintegrated again. Today, Stinnes AG is an important logistics company and has been part of the DB Group since 2002.

One day, Stinnes was in a great hurry because he absolutely had to get to Essen quickly. With squealing tires, his chauffeur reached a small train station. Stinnes bought a ticket and went straight to the stationmaster. "When will the express to Essen pass through here?" asked the industrial magnate. The stationmaster replied, "At 10:14." Stinnes followed up by asking, "What will you ask for in return, if you could stop the train so I can get on?" The clerk replied, "I don't take bribes." Stinnes urged on, but the stationmaster insisted that he would not be persuaded to stop the train for any money in the world. Eventually, the train approached. Stinnes ran to the platform and waved his hat and stick. And indeed, the train slowed down and stopped in the middle of the station. Relieved, Stinnes got on but turned to the stationmaster and said, "You see! It worked without you." "Possibly," replied the officer. He gave the signal for departure and called out to Stinnes, "the train stops here according to schedule."

Brühl Kierberg - the most beautiful station in Prussia

Brühl boasts a railway station that was once considered the most beautiful in Prussia. However, this does not refer to the station on the left bank of the Rhine - which hit the headlines in 2000 when a train derailed, killing nine people and destroying houses - but rather to the Brühl-Kierberg imperial railway station on the Eifelbahn. The Brühl-Kierberg station, built in 1875, owes its elegant design to Kaiser Wilhelm I, who visited troops in the Eifel from here and spent the night in the nearby Brühl Castle. Today, there is a restaurant with a beer garden in the station, yet, luckily, trains still stop here.

Mülheim - incompatible underground

Mülheim an der Ruhr is located between Essen and Duisburg. You can reach both cities quickly by S-Bahn. However, the main railway station has been waiting a long time for its renovation. It has an underground light rail station where light rail from Duisburg and Essen arrive. However, trams cannot pass through because the vehicles' power systems are not compatible.

Wuppertal Central Station - the classic

The Bergisch-Märkische Eisenbahn chose a classicist architectural style for its first stations. One example is the station building of Wuppertal Central Station, which was built in 1846 and is one of the oldest in Germany. At that time, this was still the station of Elberfeld. It was not until the 1920s that this town was merged with Barmen and Vohwinkel to form Wuppertal.

It is said that Kaiser Wilhelm's wife once asked Emperor when she passed the Elberfeld main station by suspended monorail, "What does 'Elberfeld HB' actually mean?" In response, the emperor said, "Hinter Barmen (behind Barmen)."

Writer Heinrich Böll (1917-1985) once wrote about Wuppertal:

"For a long time, I believed that Wuppertal consisted only of stations, lined up side by side, so as not to make the locomotive drivers get exuberant, to teach them to brake, to start up, to brake, and so on…"

Wuppertal - the Döppersberg, lions and wall

The beautiful classicistic building of Wuppertal Central Station was long disfigured by a flat roof porch, which was used by a supermarket. Additionally, there was a dingy pedestrian tunnel to the city centre, popularly known as Harnröhre (the urethra) because of its smell. This connecting passage is now history. With the completion of the Döppersberg project to redesign the area around the station, things have improved. On the upper level, meadows have been laid out in front of the station building, inviting passers-by to sit down. Two silver lions seem to walk across the grass. They are reminiscent of two bronze lions that were once placed in front of the Elberfeld town hall and could even spit fire via a gas pipeline. At some point, they stood in the way there and then embarked on an odyssey which led them to the portal of the Wuppertal Railway Directorate for a while (the two busts on their façade are, by the way, relatively new and represent the project manager and the architect of the conversion).

The upper level of the station square is bordered by a perforated natural stone wall. Coming from the city, this wall obscures the view of the historic station building a bit and seems a bit too dominant. Some people in Wuppertal have already said, "the wall has to go."

Wuppertal-Ottenbruch

Wuppertal is known for its suspension railway. However, this city, rich in industrial heritage, could offer many more transport attractions if a lack of money and ignorance of tradition had not led to the loss of many railway lines. As early as 1959, the Bergbahn (the Mountain Railway) - a rack railway in the district of Barmen - was shut down despite protests from the population. In 1987, the Wuppertal tram ran for the last time. In 1988, the railway line from Elberfeld to Cronenberg, called Samba, was closed down. In 1989, the freight traffic of the line from Vohwinkel to Solingen, called Korkenzieherbahn, was abandoned. In 1999, the Wuppertaler Nordbahn was closed down. At least a citizens' initiative, the Wuppertal Movement, was able to establish a now popular foot and cycle path on the northern railway line.

Even before the closure, the North Railway and its stations saw hardly any investment and increasingly took on a museum character. Since the trackside of Ottenbruch station (there is a restaurant in the station building of the de-commissioned station) with its antiquated platforms had not been demolished since the Second World War, it became a popular location to shoot outdoor scenes for films set in the pre-war period.

Wuppertal-Vohwinkel's underground spaces

As a local website reports (www.wuppertal-vohwin-kel.net), Vohwinkel station offers secrets invisible to today's passengers: underground spaces are located under the station. Once there were not only spacious men's and women's toilets in the basement, in which even bathtubs could be taken, but also 2500 m of heating pipes were laid, which were fed by 3 boilers in the basement. Coal was delivered on track 11 and from there it was transported to the cellar. Each platform had a luggage elevator. Pieces of luggage were transported on mobile bases through tunnel vaults to a sorting station in the cellar. This system was in operation until 1970.

Another curiosity: from the 1950s to the early 1990s, there was also track 4, which was unique in the world, a platform barber. Today, the once busy station has been transformed into an unmanned station with ticket machines and no services. So it happened that a few years ago a bank robber stormed the station's bank, which no longer exists today, with a pipe bomb.

Wuppertal Vohwinkel station

Solingen-Schaberg and the Müngstener Bridge

Since the Regionale 2006, the Schaberg stop has helped open up the area in and around the Müngstener Brückenpark. The Müngstener Bridge between Solingen and Remscheid is the highest railway bridge in Germany at 107 metres above the valley. It is held together by 934,456 rivets. Allegedly there is a rivet of pure gold among them. However, the railway's restoration teams, who regularly inspect the bridge, have still not found it.

Solingen Central Station

The station building of Solingen's main station was once an elegant fifties building. Yet, when the inter-city trains were introduced, they stopped at Solingen-Ohligs station, and the main station was only served by local and regional trains. Its somewhat remote location and the shortage of funds for the railway added to its downfall. The tower was torn down, and the station was progressively decaying. Its graffiti-smeared "Bronx ambience" almost had something worth seeing after the turn of the millennium. For the Regionale 2006, the building was closed to rail traffic and converted into a design centre. Ultimately, the Solingen-Ohligs station was renamed the main station.

Düsseldorf - the water tower

The Düsseldorf main station is a relatively sober brick building from the thirties. The 40-meter-high clock tower contains a water reservoir that was once created to fuel the steam locomotives. In 1838, the first railway in western Germany ran from Düsseldorf to Erkrath, and three years later, the line was extended to (Wuppertal) Elberfeld. Between Erkrath and Hochdahl, steam locomotives had to push the trains because the gradient is 1:30. Today, a memorial plaque identifies the line as the steepest main railway line in Europe. Parallel to it and flatter, a line leads into the Neander Valley, where important archeological discoveries of bones were made in 1856. Today, there is an S-Bahn station of the same name and a Neandertal Museum.

Düsseldorf-Benrath

The stop Düsseldorf Benrath, with its elegant brick station building dating from 1932, is the most frequented railway station in the state capital (with 30,000 travellers a day) after the central railway station. On 25 May 1965, Queen Elizabeth II of England visited Benrath Palace. The Prime Minister of North Rhine-Westphalia, Franz Meyers, received her at the station, which was ceremonially decorated for her. If Elisabeth were to come to the station portal today, she would probably feel at home linguistically because the English words 'ServiceStore' can be read above the entrance. Next to these words is a Scottish name: McDonald's.

Düsseldorf-Benrath station

Leichlingen

In the town of Leichlingen in the Rhineland, a damaged girder of a historic platform roof has been a monument at the

Bahnhofsplatz since June 2017. On a plaque at the monument the following can be read:

"On 4 October 1944, a passenger train stopping at Leichlingen station and heading for Cologne, was attacked by an American Air Force fighter bomber at about 10:20 am. The then dispatcher was still trying to get the passengers to safety in the subway. However, a heavy bomb hit the siding and destroyed parts of the train. This attack killed 20 people and many were injured. The beam of the historic platform roofing, damaged by gunfire and shell splinters, which was dismantled in 2011 for the construction of the new platform, is a historical testimony to this war event".

Beam of the historic platform at the station square

Mönchengladbach's two main stations

Mönchengladbach is the only city in Europe with two main central stations. In addition to the Mönchengladbach main station, there is also the one in Rheydt. Rheydt has belonged to Mönchengladbach since the regional reform of the 1970s, but the railway did not adjust the station name.

Mönchengladbach's main station, on the other hand, underwent a name change after the war, as the town was formerly called München-Gladbach. To avoid confusion with München (Munich), the name was changed to Mönchen-Gladbach and finally, Mönchengladbach. Despite two main train stations, there are no longer any long-distance trains stopping in the city except on Fridays and Sundays (since December 2009, there are long-distance trains to Aachen and Berlin on these days).

Hochdahl and the cable monument

The railway line from Düsseldorf to Wuppertal is one of the oldest in Germany (built between 1837 and 1841) and also contains one of the steepest ramps of any main railway line (3.3%). An information board at Hochdahl station even shows the Erkrath-Hochdahl section as the steepest main railway line in Europe. On this section of the line, there was even a cable drive from 1841-1927. A deflection pulley of the system can be admired as a technical monument at Hochdahl railway station. In 1938, it was installed in Erkrath station, but in 1986, it was moved to its technically more correct place.

11.2 Westphalia

Minden - the fortress railway station

The Cologne (formerly: Cöln)-Mindener Railway once chose a 'romantic' style with battlements and turrets similar to medieval castles for important station buildings on its lines. The island railway station of Minden, built in 1848 and situated between tracks, is one of the last architectural artifacts of this epoch. The other stations built in this style, for example Dortmund and Hamm, were later replaced by new buildings. Because the Hanoverian State Railway also ended here, the Minden station building exists twice, with a station restaurant in between, which had to close a few years ago after a fire. In the beginning, the Minden citizens only unwillingly embraced the station because it was located on the right side of the Weser, which was felt to be outside Minden. Minden, strategically located not far from the Porta Westfalica, was a border and a fortress town between Prussia and the Kingdom of Hanover. For this reason, a separate station fortress was built for the station outside the Minden fortress, which had three railway gates and a station barracks. But when Hannover became a part of Prussia in 1866, the fortress became superfluous. After the Second World War, the importance of the station increased again due to the settlement of the Federal Railway Central Office, which carried out railway engineering experiments in Minden.

Dortmund - chip shop with railway siding

After the destruction of the war, a relatively inconspicuous building for the main railway station was built in Dortmund in 1952. Due to its unremarkable architecture, the station was called a "French fries stall with siding." New construction of the station has been under discussion since the 1990s. Initially, there was a plan for a circular entertainment centre above the tracks, which was called "Ufo" because of its shape. In 2001, new plans were presented. Under the working title "3do," a Portuguese investor wanted to invest over 500 million euros in 36,000 square metres of retail space and 26,000 square metres of entertainment. However, this project also failed. In the meantime, the "French fries stall" is being modernised at a moderate expense according to the Essen model.

Huckarde

In the Dortmund district of Huckarde, the railway once lost a lawsuit against a citizen when it came to the positioning of a railway building. As if in defiance, the railway finally placed the station building in the middle of an important connecting road in 1908. This was later called "Huckarder Unikum" (Huckarder Unique). Taking advantage of the exposed location, a restaurant has been located in today's Huckarde-Nord station since 1996.

Gelsenkirchen – the decline of the West

Gelsenkirchen once had a historical railway station building dating from 1904, which was stylistically overloaded and somewhat gloomy on the inside, but with goodwill could have been transformed into a jewel. Yet, in 1982, the station building was demolished and replaced by a banal shopping mall, while access to the tracks was placed underground. This station, however, fell into disrepair so quickly that in 2005 it was presented by NRW's Minister of Construction Vesper as an example of the need for more funds. It was finally renovated for the 2006 World Cup. But for reasons similar to those in Essen, the entrance area of the main station of the "City of a Thousand Fires" (once the city's nickname because of the coal and steel industry) has been bathed in blue light.

Recklinghausen Hbf and the cigarette advertising

The main station of Recklinghausen - a post-war building with a striking clock tower, which has been rebuilt several times in the meantime - is known for two things that have disappeared. Until its renovation in 1998, a commemorative plaque for the 5000th electrified railway kilometre of the DB was found in the station. Since then, the plaque has disappeared. A Marlboro advertisement on the central platform of the main station has also disappeared. Since this was illuminated in contrast to the station sign and had a similar typeface, there was a danger that this could be misread by some passengers as a station of the neighbouring town Marl, just like Marl-Sinsen, the next station to the north.

In the station hall, however, the 'Marlboro Man' was still present. However, two letters from the red neon writing were unlit. Thus "Ma..boro" was illuminated, and confusion with Marl is again avoided. In the meantime, the Marlboro Man has also disappeared from the station hall.

Recklinghausen station

Wanne-Eickel and Heinz Rühmann

In 1975, Wanne-Eickel was incorporated in Herne. However, the station of Wanne-Eickel, not the station of Herne, has the title of Central Station. Once, Wanne was known as the "city of a thousand trains," because one of the biggest marshalling yards in Europe was located there. The group of statues called *Drei-Männer-Eck* (Three Men Corner) on the station square—which shows a railwayman, a miner, and a bargeman—reminds us of the former traffic and industrial importance of the place. The station square itself is named after the actor Heinz Rühmann (1902-1994). From 1906-1916, Rühmann's father Hermann ran a restaurant in the Wanne station. A board at the station square informs passers-by about Heinz Rühmann's years in the city (he went to grammar school in Eickel for a few years).

Wanne-Eickel station with sculpture ‚Dreimännereck'

Wanne-Eickel and the information officer

In the 1930s, the information officer Schattenberg worked at the Wanne-Eickel station, and stories are still told about him today. Once, the train with President Hindenburg, who was on his way to the Rhineland, stopped for a few minutes at Wanne station. Hindenburg stood at the window and waved.

Schattenberg saw his chance coming. He grabbed his big bronze bell, cleared the platform, and rang the bell to the President. Schattenberg, who had not served, stood at attention and greeted Hindenburg with "Herr Generalfeld-marschall (Mister Field Marshall General)." Hindenburg noticed that Schattenberg was missing an arm and asked, "Did you lose the arm in 1870/71 (in the war)?" Schattenberg answered, "Nope, on the railway forty years ago." He had lost his arm while dangerously helping trains maneuver.

Herten's missing station

In 1983, the passenger rail service of the Hamm-Osterfelder Bahn, which crosses Herten, ended. As a result, Hertens station, which was opened in 1905, was closed to passenger traffic (in the meantime, there is no longer a freight station in Herten). However, Herten (62,000 inhabitants) became something special as a result. Since then, it has been the largest town in Germany without a railway station served by rail passenger transport.

Hamm´s marshalling yard

Because of its location on the eastern edge of the Ruhr area, where freight trains to the North Sea ports and the east of Germany could be assembled, Hamm once had the largest marshalling yard in Europe. However, the station was heavily bombed during the Second World War and never again reached its pre-war significance due to a reorientation of the traffic flows, the production focus, and the logistics. However, the neo-baroque station building, built in 1920, looks more like that of a spa town. Only the figures of a miner and a wire-puller next to the station clock above the entrance allude to the once important trades made in the town. In the mid-nineties, the station building was renovated in an exemplary manner and received a European monument protection prize.

Hamm and the little hunger

In the eighties, the Hindu priest Sri Paskaran, who had come to Germany from Sri Lanka as a civil war refugee, travelled by train from Berlin to Paris. Since he felt hungry after several hours of travel, Paskaran got off the train in Hamm to get something to eat. He interpreted the interruption of the journey as a sign from the gods to open a Hindu temple in this city. Additionally, in other respects, this choice was fitting. The station is painted in the temple colours red-white, the pattern in the city coat of arms is also red-white, and the landmark Hamm´s is a glass elephant. In the beginning, Paskaran had only a small basement altar. However, in July 2002, Paskaran opened the largest Hindu temple on the European mainland in Hamm.

Bielefeld and the bicycles

Münster is known as the bicycle capital of Germany. The city has Germany's largest bicycle station at the train station (3300 parking spaces). However, it was not Münster, but rather Bielefeld - once home to important bicycle manufacturers - that opened Germany's first bicycle station in 1992 (390 parking spaces). Today, there are 70 bike stations in NRW alone, with a total of over 20,000 parking spaces. The Netherlands is the only place with more (around 100 bike stations).

☞In 1994, the Bielefeld conspiracy, a satire that cast doubt on the existence of the city, was launched. All references to the existence of Bielefeld are part of a large-scale conspiracy. Since many ICE trains pass through the city and stop at the station, some travellers of the conspiracy theory wonder if all this is just scenery.

Bielefeld and the missing link

Strangely enough, there is no underground access to the Bielefeld train station from the main train station in Bielefeld. Rather, one has to go to the surface and walk a few meters before one gets to the station. The missing underground connection is explained by massive world war bunkers that are located between the city train station and the main station.

The light rail entrance of the main station is called Tüte (bag) by locals and was at times a social hotspot.

Altenbeken - the golden viaduct

The railway station of Altenbeken in the Egge Mountains in eastern Westphalia was once an important railway junction, and Altenbeken still sees itself as a railway town today. The construction of the Bekeviaduct, the largest sand-lime brick bridge in Europe (begun in 1851), has contributed to this. At the inauguration of the viaduct in 1853, the Prussian King Wilhelm IV said: "I thought I would find a golden bridge because it cost so many thalers (former coins of the German Empire)." On the Altenbeker coat of arms, one can see a golden viaduct against a blue background. Since December 2002, the arches of the "golden bridge" are illuminated at night.

Hagen - last station concourse in Westphalia

Hagen has the reputation of being one of the ugliest cities in Germany. However, the main station does not contribute to this belief. The tracks are covered by a two-bay platform hall, built in 1910, which is the only remaining platform hall in Westphalia and the Ruhr area. The station building has a similar structure to a church. In 1911, the Hagen Patron of the Arts Karl Ernst Osthaus had a stained-glass window above the main entrance decorated with a stained glass painting by the Dutch artist Thron Prikker (1868-1932). At the beginning of the 20th century, important artistic developments (Hagener Impulse) emanated from Hagen; the stained-glass window reminds us of this in the grey present. From autumn 2004 to spring 2006, the station concourse was renovated. Passengers had to find their way under scaffolding and covers, and the hall soon had the nickname "Grusel Grotto (Scary Grotto)."

Hagen main station

Hagen-Hohenlimburg

While Hagen itself does not exactly have the reputation of a tourist town, Hohenlimburg, which was incorporated in 1975, was once considered a Westphalian Heidelberg because of its location between the river and the mountainside. Even today, many Hohenlimburgers have not come to terms with this incorporation and continue to fight for their independence.

The Hohenlimburgers were also not happy for a long time about the fact that a railway line cut the town in half and created an annoying traffic barrier. Many said, "10 years in Hohenlimburg, five of them before railway barriers." In May 2009, a car and pedestrian bridge was finally opened at Hohenlimburg railway station. The bridge was provided with a coat of arms, not the coat of arms of the city of Hagen, but rather that of Hohenlimburg, which is typical for the location.

Dülmen-Buldern and the great Bomberg

In Dülmen, there is a pub at the station called "Toller Bomberg." There was also an Intercity train once called like that. How is it that a character from a picaresque novel is so honoured by the railway?

In Josef Winckler's (1881-1966) successful novel *The Great Bomberg* (750,000 copies sold), the baron is an avid train user. The railway line from Münster to the Ruhr area runs past his castle in Bullbergen, but there is no railway station nearby. Thus, Bomberg, who often stays in Münster, helps himself to the annoyance of the railway by repeatedly pulling the emergency brake. He hands the conductor the penalty due for this with the remark "We'll see who can stand it longer, the taxman or me." Once even a British aristocrat was sitting in a train coming from Hanover when Bomberg pulled the emergency brake, urinated on a telegraph pole in Bullbergen, got back on the train to get into the waiting carriage in Dülmen. The railway was so embarrassed by this that it finally came to its senses and had a railway station built in Bullbergen. Bomberg and the local population celebrated the opening of the smallest railway station in Westphalia.

So much for the story. But the novel had real examples. Bomberg's real name was Gisbert Freiherr von Romberg (1839-1997) and Bullbergen meant Buldern. The castle in Buldern, which is now a district of Dülmen, today houses a boarding school and thus provides for the corresponding rail traffic.

Pub at the station

Selm-Beifang and the emergency brake

At the beginning of the 20th century, the town of Selm on the northern edge of the Ruhr area grew rapidly from 2000 to 10,000 inhabitants as a result of industrialisation and coal mining. Yet, by 1926, the coal mine was closed down. This was an economic catastrophe for the village, and many miners had to look for work elsewhere. Many continued to live in Selm and commuted by train. Often, emergency stops at the level of the Beifanger Weg because the miners who lived in this part of the village and were tired from their work did not want to take the long way from Selm station to Selm. Even the railway police did not manage to prevent these emergency stops. Therefore, the railway finally came to its senses, and in 1946, they set up another stop: today's Beifang station. Since then, it has been nicknamed "Bahnhof Not-bremse' (Emergency brake station)."

Münster main station and the bicycles

Münster is the bicycle capital of Germany with the highest percentage of cyclists of all major cities (about 30%). With so many cyclists, it is not surprising that Münster also has Germany's largest train station bicycle station: a striking triangular building with over 3,300 bicycle stands. Still, many bicycles are also parked in the streets near the station.

Münster main station and the reconstruction

Münster's central station is an important railroad junction with 70,000 passengers daily and nine railroad lines that lead from here in all directions. After the destruction of the historic station building in the Second World War, a relatively sober style building was constructed in the post-war period. For this reason, there had been plans for a more representative entrance to the city for several years. Construction began at the end of 2014, and the building was put into operation in 2017. However, the platforms and the northern underpass were already renovated in 2009-2013, which was urgently needed, as there were no lifts or escalators. Their absence was also revealed in a tragic accident in July 2009. 79-year-old legal scholar Werner Hoppe was pulled down by the weight of his trolley, stumbled on the stairs, and fell to the tracks. He suffered a head injury, which led to his death shortly afterward.

12. Hesse

12.1 South Hesse

The Frankfurt bang

Frankfurt's main railway station was opened on a greenfield site on 18.8.1888. It was regarded as a monumental event, with which the rich trading and banking city wanted to underpin its role as a regional traffic junction, also in relation to cities such as Offenbach. At the same time, the city wanted to outdo Berlin, which had been the capital of the regained German Empire since 1871 and had become a competitor to Frankfurt. The city's advertisement seeking potential architects, therefore, stated, "It is important [to us] to create something unique, to define a type of central station that will surpass the completed station buildings in terms of its mighty dimensions." In the 1960s and 1970s, the station, which was only slightly destroyed in World War II, was mainly extended in depth. S-Bahn and U-Bahn lines and an underground shopping level were built. However, those were not the only new construction projects. Under the platforms, there is also a system of post and baggage tunnels, called "Katakomben" (Catacombs) by the railways.

Wiesbaden Main Station and the Emperor

Wiesbaden was a noble spa town before the First World War and was considered a "Pensionopolis" (Metropolis of Retirees) because of the industrialists who settled there in old age. Emperor Wilhelm II also often stayed in Wiesbaden. Every spring, the city became the imperial residence. This meant that a representative railway station had to be built, and, as with other important buildings of the time, Wilhelm intervened in the plans and implemented his own architectural ideas. The station (opened in 1906) was pompous, but unlike Hamburg's main station—which was built at the same time and has a similar clock tower - it did not adopt new architectural trends such as Art Nouveau. Additionally, part of the valley slope of Melonenberg had to be removed for the construction of the station. This became so expensive due to the slope's construction that it was nicknamed "Millionenberg (millions-mountain)."

Bad Homburg

Additionally, Bad Homburg was once the summer residence of the German Emperor Wilhelm II and a popular spa resort for the nobility. The station building, built in 1907, was to be correspondingly representative to its anticipated visitors. A separate royal residence was built for the emperor, and Wilhelm II personally influenced its design. He wanted the building to be in a Renaissance style and to take up motifs from the town of Rothenburg ob der Tauber.

After the First World War, noble spa guests were absent, and Bad Homburg's importance as a world spa was lost. The railway station was not destroyed in the Second World War, and after the end of the war, the station served as a residence for the military governors Eisenhower and Clay. During this period, a military train stood ready for operation on the platform, and for the occupying powers, direct trains ran to Berlin and Bremerhaven (where US ships landed). Today, the Fürstenbahnhof is a music venue, while the main station building is currently being renovated after a fire.

Friedberg and Elvis Presley

The American singer Elvis Presley (1935-1977) did his military service in Friedberg in Hesse from 1958 to 1960. On the morning of October 1, 1958, a troop transporter with Elvis on board arrived in Bremerhaven. When Elvis—along with the other US soldiers—boarded a train to Hesse at Columbuskaje, 5000 fans were on hand. That evening, hundreds of fans waited at Friedberg station to see the star get off the train. However, the train passed through and only stopped two km later at the loading ramp of the Ray Barracks. There were already 50 radio, television, and press reporters posted there, yet, only 20 fans saw Elvis get off the train with 1400 other US soldiers. Elvis was stationed in Friedberg until March 2, 1960, but during this time, he lived in Bad Nauheim.

Death in Nidda

On 19 October 1939, Emanuel Eckstein bled to death in the train station of Nidda. The 66-year-old Jewish man came from this town but had moved to Frankfurt with his family half a year earlier. During his visit to his hometown, he encountered a hostile atmosphere. A mob chased him through the city, and stones flew. Bleeding, Eckstein arrived at the train station and dragged himself into the third class waiting room. However, instead of the cup of coffee he requested, he received a punch in the chest and died soon after.

Messel and the bell

At Messel station—opened in 1857 and constructed as part of the Rhein-Main Bahn (Mainz-Darmstadt-Aschaffenburg) of the Hessische Ludwigsbahn)—a bell used to ring 20 times before the trains left. The bell was rung repeatedly to inform workers of the nearby Messel pit of the impending departure. Today, the Messel Pit is a UNESCO World Natural Heritage Site because of the important fossil discoveries. The former railway station bell is now in use at a cemetery in Pfungstadt.

12.2 Central Hesse

Marburg's champagne station

When Marburg's railway station was rebuilt between 1907 and 1909, it was still far outside the gates of the city.

How was the peripheral location in the north of the city able to assert itself against a location closer to the city (Weidenhausen), which was also being discussed? The website of the city of Marburg provides information about this under the heading 'Secrets' (www.marburg.de):

The local landowner Hofmann invited those involved in the decision, including representatives of the city parliament and the Main-Weser-Bahn, to a relaxed dinner in a Marburg restaurant. The choice of location finally fell on a piece of land that belonged to Hofmann. Since then, the station has been nicknamed the Champagne Station.

The choice of location was not completely absurd because the alternative location Weidenhausen was later repeatedly affected by flooding. Nevertheless, there are now plans to build a station closer to the city for the numerous commuters (Marburg station is frequented by 12,000 travellers daily).

Wetzlar's lost Art Nouveau station

Until 1985, Wetzlar station had one of the few art nouveau station buildings in the area of the Deutsche Bahn. Yet, in 1985, the culturally and historically valuable building, which was erected in 1917, was demolished during the modernization of the signal box technology. The follow-up building, opened in 1986, contains the new central signal box and is otherwise characterised by banal block architecture. In contrast to its predecessor, it did not age with dignity, but increasingly became an eyesore of the city. Nevertheless, modernisation measures have now been started on the railway facilities and the station square.

While Wetzlar has a historic old town and a new railway station, in Giessen, it is almost the other way round. The old town of Giessen was destroyed in the war, but the station was preserved. Today, the city has the most beautiful station building in Central Hesse.

Arfurt´s corrugated iron station

Arfurt is a district of the Hessian town of Runkel with about 1000 inhabitants and a very elementary railway station. In its modesty, however, it is still something special. The station has a small wagon-shaped waiting room and is the only corrugated iron station in Germany. The website *http://arfurt.com/arfurter_bahnhof.htm* says that a model of the station is in the Deutsches Museum in Munich and that the nickname "Wellblechhausen (Corrugated Iron House)" for Arfurt is derived from the station.

Limburg South - only ICE's

The ICE station Limburg Süd is the only German station where only ICE trains stop. However, most ICE trains speed up to 300 km/h. This is not the only reason why Limburg Süd is not a station that invites you to stay. In the station itself, there are no shops and not even public toilets (except in the adjacent parking garage), despite the planned commercial areas. There are no trains from Limburg South to the Limburg train station, and a shuttle bus service between the two stations has been discontinued. Additionally, there is no direct road connection to it, although the ICE station is located in the Eschhofen district.

12.3 Northern Hesse

Kassel-Wilhelmshöhe - the palace of a thousand winds

In 1991, the Kassel-Wilhelmshöhe station, newly built as part of the high-speed Hanover-Würzburg line, was put into operation. In light of the numerous changes to the plan launched by the railway company, the original team of architects quit, and the result was an unsatisfactory combination of different approaches. The platforms are located at a low level and are considered so draughty that the station was nicknamed "Palace of a Thousand Winds." The forecourt is also draughty, as it is located in the fresh air corridor of the winds from Wilhelmshöhe. The English Wikipedia page about the station (but not the German version) contains the following anecdote. When the then German President Richard von Weizsäcker (*1920) inaugurated the station in May 1991, he had some urgent business to attend to but could not find a toilet in the confusing station. So he allegedly had to relieve himself on a wall, shielded by bodyguards.

Kassel main station and the neophytes

Kassel's main station has been developed as a cultural station since 1995 and is regularly included in the Dokumenta art exhibition. On the occasion of the 10th Dokumenta 1997, the Austrian artist Lois Weinberger planted track 1 with neophytes. The track area has a dry and warm climate, so that plants from the south and from outside Europe (via the gardens) spread along the railway lines. Examples of plants include the Canadic goldenrod (Solidago) in the track area, the butterfly bush (Buddleia) - which comes from China and colonises fallow land in large cities and railway embankments - or the Russian giant hogweed (Heracleum Mantegazzianum).

Fulda and the span poles

Thanks to long-distance commuters (Frankfurt) and good ICE train connections, Fulda station has a considerable number of 20,000 journeys per day, which is remarkable for the size of the city. A special feature of the station is the number of transformer masts of the 110 kV traction power line, which runs along the railway line. There are 30 span poles, including one as a roof stand on a storage shed. According to Wikipedia, this is the largest number of successive span poles in Germany, possibly even worldwide.

Africa - via Bebra

The north Hessian Bebra was once an important railway junction. Even after the Second World War, Bebra still had this function, as it became a border crossing station, and Kassel was connected to the north-south traffic via Bebra. In a popular film of the 1950s, the comedian Heinz Erhardt (1909-1979) said "What? You still want to get to Africa? But first you have to change in Bebra." However, the new Hanover-Würzburg line, opened in 1991, passed Bebra, and it lost its role as a railway junction.

Eschwege and the 8960 days

In 1985, the city railway station of the 20,000 inhabitant city of Eschwege, located on the eastern edge of Hesse, was closed down. After that, only the station Eschwege West, located far from the city centre, offered rail connections. On 12 December 2009, however, the inner-city station and the associated line were reactivated. Eschweger calculated that 8960 rail-free days had come to an end. The number of passengers promptly doubled. In November 2013, the successful station even received the European Rail Award in London.

13. Rhineland-Palatinate

Bad Ems and the Emperor

Wilhelm I. (1797-1888), King of Prussia beginning in 1861 and German Emperor starting in 1871, often stayed in Bad Ems looking for a cure. In the 19th century, the place was a world spa and summer residence of Russian tsars. To prevent the monarchs arriving by train from standing in the rain on the platform, the modestly sized station was converted into a station concourse, the smallest currently in Germany.

Ludwigshafen (Rhine) - once the most modern station

Ludwigshafen's main railway station, when rebuilt in 1969 (replacing a terminus station) was considered the most modern railway station in Europe. After the war, however, Ludwigshafen was primarily designed as a city suitable for motor vehicles. For example, a motorway crosses the station, which is located somewhat away from the city centre and has two track levels that converge. However, what was once modern now looks worn out. Additionally, a more centrally located station has been built closer to the city centre as part of the Rhine-Neckar urban railway. Today, there are no more open ticket counters, no more seats at the main station, and recently, the last toilet was closed. Therefore, what was once the most modern railway station is increasingly becoming the most rotten station in Europe.

Montabaur railway station

The new ICE Frankfurt-Cologne line runs for a short distance into Rhineland-Palatinate, and the state insisted on a traffic stop, even though there are no major cities nearby. Therefore, the tranquil town of Montabaur (14,000 inhabitants) received an ICE stop. But since not all express trains can stop there, the station of Montabaur is, at the same time, one of only four

- Limburg-South (the only station where only ICE's stop), Allersberg, and Kinding - in Germany, which trains can pass with 300 km/h. However, over time passenger numbers in Montabaur have increased and close to the station a factory outlet centre has been built. Montabaur is today the town in Germany with the highest density of Bahncard 100 railway reduction card owners.

Mainz and the death of the poet

The British poet Roden Noel (*1834) died in 1894 when, while travelling by train to his sister-in-law living in Stuttgart, he suffered a heart attack while changing trains at Mainz main station. He is buried at Mainz main cemetery.

Mainz Hbf

Mainz main station and the cameras

The main station of Mainz was the first German station where face recognition software was tested. Here, several escalators lead to the tracks, which was ideal for filming people. A computer compares the faces captured by a camera with wanted pictures.

Rolandseck and art

The railway station of Rolandseck (district of Remagen) was opened in 1858 and not only has a representative station building but also offers a beautiful view over the Rhine and Siebengebirge. In the 19th century, many celebrities came here for a rendezvous, including Kaiser Wilhelm II, the English Queen Victoria, the German Prime Minister Otto von Bismarck, philosopher Friedrich Nietzsche, the Brothers Grimm, and musicians such as Johannes Brahms, Clara Schuman, and Franz Liszt. The French poet Guillaume Apollinaire and the Irish playwright George Bernhard Shaw not only stayed here but also wrote about the railway station. In September 2007, the magnificent station building became part of the Arp Museum Bahnhof Rolandseck, even though the sculptors Hans Arp (1886-1966) and Sophie Taeuber-Arp (1889-1943) had no connection to the station.

View of the Rhine from Rolandseck

14. Saarland

Saarbrücken main station - special train to Pankow

In 1983, the singer Udo Lindenberg (*1946) had a surprise success with the song "Sonderzug nach Pankow (Special Train to Pankow)," which pokes fun at the GDR leadership. However, the GDR surprisingly responded positively to the jabs and invited the singer to a concert in the GDR.

The video for the song was shot by Lindenberg in the main station of Saarbrücken. This "office block with station function," completed in 1971, was still considered modern at the time, but with its brown tiles, the station looked like it could have been located in the GDR. Coincidentally, General Secretary of the GDR Erich Honecker came from the Saarland. After the turn of the millennium, the interior design of the station was no longer regarded as modern, and in 2007, it was modernised under the working title "Euro-Bahnhof" during the opening of the new East French TGV line. The Austrian writer Joseph Roth (1894-1939) once wrote that "Saarbrücken is the saddest station, which I have ever got of a train at." He probably had not made it to Völklingen by then.

Völklingen - Apocalypse Now

The Saarland industrial town of Völklingen has the reputation of being "Germany's ugliest town." The decline of the city centre, in particular, is apparent when one arrives at the railway station. Saarlander Peter Gitzinger described the station forecourt in his 2010 book *111 Places in Saarland You Have to See*. From the back of the station, one has an unobstructed view of the rusty former steelworks Völklinger Hütte, which despite its bizarre appearance, is now on the UNESCO list of World Cultural Heritage Sites. In Gitzinger's opinion, the "complete horror" grips you on the front, the two concrete tracks of the southern tangent spread "an atmosphere that you normally only know from post-apocalyptic horror scenarios."

Losheim am See and the railway post museum

After the First World War, Losheim (located on the Merzig (Saar)-Büschfeld railway line) became part of the Saar area border station. This which was separated from the rest of Germany and became a Prussian Rhine province with its own customs office. After the Second World War, however, the low passenger numbers led to a gradual closure of the line, and passenger traffic was completely stopped in May 1962. In 1987, freight traffic was also discontinued, but this was reintroduced in 2007 due to the request of a wood-processing company located on the route. Since 1982, there has also been a museum railway service and a railway museum at Losheim am See station. When the German Railways stopped the railway mail service in 1997, the Arbeits-gemeinschaft Bahnpost (Railway Post Committee), a group of collectors and railway mail drivers, decided to purchase three railway mail coaches and park them in Losheim am See. Thus the station became Germany's only railway post museum. Every year on the second weekend in August, a Railway Post Festival is held there.

Beckingen and the bullet holes

From 2009 to 2010, the station building of the Beckingen station, located on the Moselle line between Trier and Saarbrücken, was converted into a cultural and natural railway station.

Built in 1868 in the neo-Gothic style, the station building was in urgent need of renovation. At the beginning of the renovation, bullet holes from the Second World War were still visible. The 20 m high station tower, which was destroyed in the Second World War and resembled the towers of the old Saarbrücken main station, was rebuilt during the construction work.

Bexbach station and the 111 places

In his book *111 Places in Saarland You Have to See*, author Peter Gitzinger lists Bexbach station as the only railway station. He justifies his claim by stating that Bexbach is the oldest preserved railway station building in Saarland. When it was built in 1849, Bexbach was the border station between Bavaria (to which the Palatinate belonged at the time) and Prussia. Later, the station retained its strategic importance, as it was a deployment area for the Franco-Prussian War of 1870/71, and troop trains were loaded and unloaded here during World War I.

15. Baden-Württemberg

15.1 Baden

The Cuckoo Clock

In the middle of the 19th century, the Black Forest cuckoo clock industry was in crisis, partly due to cheap imports from America. Robert Gerwig (1820-1885), director of the Grand Ducal Baden Clockmaker School in Furtwangen, therefore announced a competition for a contemporary design for cuckoo clocks. Coincidentally, the versatile Gerwig later became an important railway engineer who designed the Black Forest Railway, the Höllental Railway, and the northern ramp of the Gotthard route.

Gerwig's competition was won by the station architect Friedrich Eisenlohr (1805-1854), who designed several of the first station buildings in the Baden area between Offenburg and Freiburg, with a clock in the form of a "Bahnhäusle (Railway House Clock)." Eisenlohr had also designed station attendant's houses with protruding roofs, which were inspired by the Black Forest farmhouse. The "Bahnhäusle Clock," still the basic model of the cuckoo clock today, finally helped the Black Forest clock industry out of the crisis and become a lasting export success.

Heidelberg and the first railway station bookstore

Heidelberg has a central station which was built in the 1950s. However, this station did not replace a station destroyed in the war but rather took over the role of the city's most important station from a smaller one closer to the city centre. It was in this first Heidelberg station that the first German railway station bookshop was founded in 1854. A well-travelled brother-in-law told the Heidelberg university bookseller Carl Schmitt that a newspaper station had been located in the Euston Station in London since 1848 and that the Hachette Company, the largest book publisher in France, had been operating station bookshops in Paris since 1853. The Heidelberg booksellers, however, turned up their noses at Schmitt's decision to sell books in a station. Even today, there is a Karl Schmitt bookstore in Heidelberg's main station. Today, the Karl Schmitt chain ranks fourth in terms of sales among railway station bookstores in Germany.

Pforzheim central station - the Goldstadt station

In February 1945, 28,000 hundredweights of explosive and incendiary bombs from 370 British fighter planes fell on the jewelry city of Pforzheim, which was suspected to be home to the arms industry (fuses and precision instruments). As a result, a heat storm raged through the city. Even in Tübingen, 60 kilometers away, the glowing red sky could be seen. Burnt stationery from Pforzheim was blown all the way to Stuttgart and Lake Constance. The city burned for nine days, 20,000 people died, and 98% of the buildings in the inner-city area were destroyed, which was more than in any other German city. While the ruins of an architecturally once beautiful Pforzheim were buried in a nearby mountain, the city was rebuilt in the 1950s in a functional but faceless style. When the railway company planned to replace the old, destroyed station with a new building that was as modest as possible, many Pforzheimers felt bad that their city should be rebuilt in such an unpleasing architectural style. As a result, the "Pforzheim station war" ensued. In the end, the federal railway and the city found a compromise. The architect Conradi designed a modern station with an elegant glass front. In the entrance hall, a metal sculpture by the artist Joseph Karl Huber with the theme "Goldstadt an der Schwarzwaldpforte (Gold City at the Black Forest Gate)" was installed. The canopy made of steel was covered with gold anodised panels, in which 36 recessed lights created an artificial sky. The local press celebrated the "station with a golden roof." And so, the Pforzheimers were able to alleviate the pain resulting from the loss of their cityscape, at least at this construction site.

Mannheim - the city of inventors

Besides Stuttgart, Mannheim also claims the title of the city where the car was invented. Mannheim's Carl Benz was a few months ahead of Daimler with his vehicle. However, Benz's automobile only had three wheels. The two-wheeler, in turn, was invented by Drais from Karlsruhe, also in Mannheim. Today, there is a large bicycle station near the Mannheim main station. By the way, the Benz from Baden and the Swabian Daimler never met each other. Today, it would be easier to arrange a meeting between the pair meeting since the Stuttgart - Mannheim line was opened in 1987. Upon the line's opening, the satirical magazine *Titanic* proposed the following question: "Over 4 billion DM invested just to be in Mannheim 40 minutes earlier? The same could have been achieved at no cost by letting the trains leave 40 minutes earlier."

The Karlsruhe Model

Karlsruhe has also written transport history, but one which is related to the railway. Karlsruhe has a well-preserved art nouveau railway station, which was opened in 1913. However, it is not the architecture of this rather inconspicuous station (once called Villa Duckdich) that is special, but the Karlsruhe S-Bahn system, which is copied by other cities as the "Karlsruhe Model." Karlsruhe was a pioneer in linking urban tram lines with the railway network of the surrounding area. The driving force was the former head of the transport company, Dieter Ludwig. Ludwig once shared the story of an old mother who gave him a euro in out of gratitude for allowing her to now travel anywhere.

Constance and Lake Constance

The railway station of Constance with its access routes is located between the old town and the lake. How was it possible to find space for the train on the densely built up shore? As in Lindau, land was gained by filling up the lake. And so the station tower in Konstanz almost looks like a lighthouse, which can be found in the Lindau harbour.

Baden-Baden and the opera

The noble spa town of Baden-Baden has a through station in the district of Oos (8000 travellers/day). Additionally, there was once a representative station in the city centre. However, the last trains departed from this station in 1977. After that, the station served as a casino for a few years until 1998, when the block-like festival hall behind the station was opened. Since then, the station building has served as the entrance to the Festspielhaus (Festival theater).

Rheinfelden (Baden) - on the wrong side?

When one gets off at Rheinfelden (Baden) station, they get the feeling that the station building is on the wrong side of the tracks. It is on the south side facing the Rhine, but the city centre is on the north side. The reason for this is surprising. When the station was built, a Rheinfelden in Baden did not even exist. The station was rather built with regard to the passenger potential in the Swiss Rheinfelden, which is located on the other side of the Rhine. Once the railway station came into existence, it attracted economic activity on the Baden side. Over the decades, a corresponding town was formed on the northern side (away from where the station faces) since there was building land mainly north of the tracks.

Kehl and the memorial plaque

In the 1930s, the border station at Kehl was an important station for those seeking safe exile. A plaque in the station commemorates two poets and thinkers who left the German Reich by rail from here: Heinrich Mann (22 February 1933) and Sigmund Freud (5 June 1938), who went into exile in London after the Annexation of Austria.

Radolfzell and the most beautiful waiting room

The Radolfzell station does not have a real waiting hall. Yet, the town on Lake Constance prides itself on having the "most beautiful waiting area in Germany." However, the "waiting area" was actually a reference to the Radolfzell city garden near the station by the Swabian writer Ludwig Finckh (1876-1964).

Orschweier and the railway revolution

A commemorative plaque was unveiled at Orschweier station on 23 September 2008. It commemorates the Orschweier railway revolt that had taken place exactly 160 years earlier. During the Baden Revolution of 1848/49, Orschweier citizens had destroyed train tracks. At that time, Baden was influenced by France and was a democratic pioneer in Germany. Revolutionaries had proclaimed a republic in Lörrach, and the citizens of Orschweier destroyed the tracks and a railway bridge so that North Baden troops could not quickly get through to Lörrach. The transport of troops was stopped, but pioneers repaired the track so that the revolution could be put down.

Stuttgart main station - the basilica

Stuttgart's main station, designed by Paul Bonatz and opened in 1922, has the atmosphere of a basilica with its shell limestone façade. This is particularly noticeable in the exit area. The Russian writer Ilja Ehrenburg (1891-1967), who stopped here in 1922, described it as a 'temple of an unknown cult.' The entrance to the Intercity Hotel in the station is reminiscent of a sacristy door. Coincidentally, the predecessor hotel was the first hotel to open in a German railway station in 1927. The main station is relatively close to the city centre. However, it is already the third incarnation of Stuttgart Central Station. Each time the station was built, it moved a little further out of the city centre. With the controversial Stuttgart 21 project—whose completion is not yet foreseeable (2025?)—the station is again moving. Yet, this time it will move underground and become a through station. The currently preserved station building, however, will remain. On the station's tower, the Mercedes star rotates and is visible from afar. This is also a sign that Stuttgart is a car city because the four-wheeled car, the truck, and the motorcycle (as well as the taximeter and the spark plug) were invented here, and well-known car manufacturers are located here.

Reutlingen and List

The economist, pioneer of the customs union, and railway pioneer Friedrich List was born in Reutlingen, Swabia, in 1789, and died by suicide in Kufstein in 1846. Posthumously, he received many honours: several streets are named after him, stamps were issued for his 200th birthday, and several monuments were created. As the initiator of the railway Leipzig-Dresden, List is honoured by a bust in Leipzig central station and by a monument at Friedrich List-Platz near Dresden central station. In Kufstein, a big marble monument commemorates him. In Reutlingen, his hometown, a bronze statue - the first independent work (1854) by the sculptor Gustav Adolph Kietz (1824-1908) - at Bahnhofsplatz honours him.

Plochingen and the cheese wagon

In 1894, a freight train loaded with cheese loaves overturned in Plochingen, today an important Stuttgart S-Bahn station. Economical as Swabians tend to be, the people of Plochingen immediately took care of the load. Since then, the Plochingeners have been nicknamed Käsräuber (cheese robbers).

Bertolt Brecht - made in Pfullingen (train station)

The writer Bertolt Brecht was born on 10 February 1898 in Augsburg. However, the city of Pfullingen in Wurttemberg also claims the author for itself with the slogan "Bertold Brecht: made in Pfullingen." One reason for Pfullingen's claim stems from the fact that Brecht's parents, Berthold Friedrich Brecht and Wilhelmine Sophie Brezing, validated their marriage on 15 May 1897 at the Pfullinger registry office. The father of the bride was the head of the Pfullingen station. Thus, the wedding was celebrated in the station building, and the young couple spent their wedding night in the station apartment. Nine months later, Brecht was born in Augsburg, even though he was conceived in Pfullingen train station.

The spätzle (pasta) station

Trochtelfingen is located in the Swabian Alb (not far from Burladingen) and is the headquarters of the pasta producer Alb-Gold, which is known for its "Original Swabian Spätzle" (a type of egg-based pasta from Swabia). A railway line runs past the customer centre of Alb-Gold, which is just outside the town. On 25 March 2006, the station "Trochtelfingen Alb-Gold" was put into operation there. Soon after, it had the nickname "Spätzleshaltestelle (Spätzle (pasta) Station)."

Killer and whips

In the Swabian Alb, there is a railway station, where the word "Killer" is attached to the facade. As if that were not enough, in the rooms of the station building, there is also a whip museum. Killer is the name of a Swabian village, which today belongs to Burladingen and is still served by the Hohenzollern state railway. The Hohenzollerische Landesbahn did not need a station building in the village anymore, so in 1993, a whip museum was established in the station. The harsh climate of the Alb and the narrowness of the valley made farming in Killer not very productive. In search of another industry, the population specialized in the production of whips. When horses were still an important means of transport, 5000 whips were produced in the village every day. Overall, half of all whips in Germany came from Killer.

Altbach and the people mover

The first PeopleMover crossing railway tracks was installed on 19 December 2006 at Altbach station (Esslingen district), which is located on the Fils valley railway line Stuttgart-Ulm. On the occasion of the inauguration, the mayor of the town had created the Swabian-sounding term "Leutelupfer (People Lobber)" for the elevator system. However, some users misused the leisurely ride of the elevator car in the horizontal direction to relieve themselves. Thus, the Leutelupfer was characterized by a certain scent soon after it was put into operation.

Heilbronn main station and Joseph Beuys

In spring 2016, I visited the exhibition 'Joseph Beuys and Italy' at the Kunsthalle Vogelmann in Heilbronn. What I did not know at that time is that Joseph Beuys' 'first art action' took place in Heilbronn's main station in 1945.

As a returning soldier after the end of the Second World War, Joseph Beuys (1921-1986) arrived at Heilbronn main station one evening. Here an official was to hand him the papers he needed to continue his journey. However, the official refused and, therefore, Beuys would have had to spend the night in the waiting room of the destroyed station. In response, Beuys punched the official and switched off the main power in the station. In the chaos that ensued, Beuys managed to steal the necessary papers and continue his journey. Beuys later referred to the act as *Aktion Hauptstrom* (Action Main Power), his first art action, and this is what his saying '"The Mysteries are Happening at the Central Station" refers to.

Today, around 12,000 people use Heilbronn's main train station every day. However, the city regrets the lack of long-distance trains. For the Federal Horticultural Show 2019, however, individual Intercity express trains stopped here, and due to the closure of the Stuttgart-Mannheim high-speed line from April-October 2020, there will be further ICE or IC stops during this period.

Öhringen Central Station

When Öhringen was connected to the Karlsruhe-Heilbronn light rail system in December 2005, there were suddenly three rail stops in the city. Therefore, the city applied to rename the formerly only station into the main station. In December 2008, this became reality, and the small town had its main station (Hauptbahnhof). It does not seem as important as it sounds because in the summer of the same year, DB informed the city that it wanted to sell this station.

The station and the assassin

Next to the platform of track 2 (trains towards Ulm) of the station of the East Württemberg town of Königsbronn is a steel monument to a man who took the train from here to Munich on August 5, 1939, but never returned to his town. The monument commemorates Georg Elser (1903-1945), who left here to prepare an assassination attempt on Hitler in Munich.

Hitler was supposed to give a speech in the Bürgerbräukeller on the evening of 8 November 1939. Elser placed a time bomb in a column of the speaker's stand, which he had hollowed out in nightly detail work. The bomb detonated exactly as planned at 21:20, and eight people died. However, Hitler, who was actually supposed to be speaking at that time, was not among them. He had already left the hall earlier because he had to travel back to Berlin by train instead of by plane due to bad weather. If the assassination had been successful, world history would have taken a different course, and perhaps, the death of millions of people in the World War would have been prevented. Georg Elser was arrested at the border in Konstanz a short time later while attempting to escape to Switzerland. In April 1945, shortly before the end of the Second World War, Elser was executed in Dachau concentration camp by a shot in the neck. After the war, numerous squares and streets were named after Elser. In May 2009, the artist Friedrich Frankowitsch began work on a monument to Elser, which, however, was not completed by the 70th anniversary of the attack. It was finally erected at Königsbronn station in April 2010. One of the artistic freedoms Frankowitsch took was by adding a briefcase from with dynamite is sticking out. However, Elser travelled to Munich with a chest and without dynamite. Furthermore, the statue shows five fingers on each hand, but Elser only had four on his right hand.

Bad Saulgau and the Kleberexpress

The traditional Hotel Kleber-Post stands at the train station of the Upper Swabian health resort Bad Saulgau. The horses were changed here at the time of Thurn & Taxis. The hotel was operated by the Kleber family until the 11th generation and the last generations were great rail enthusiasts. As early as 1937, Fritz Kleber turned to the Reichsbahn to create an express train connection from Munich to Freiburg via Bad Saulgau. The railway agreed, but the annexation of Austria in 1938 led to new priorities. In 1954, his son Herman Kleber finally managed to set up a pair of express trains from Munich to Freiburg. Grandson Andreas Kleber, born in 1947, also became a railroad fan, he even passed an exam for a driver. However, he was almost too late for the master kitchen exam because the locomotive had cylinder damage. But because he could lend a hand himself, he still got there. On October 10, 1980, the express train from Saulgau to Kißlegg was used by Andreas Kleber and his fiancé as the wedding train `IC Johanna Kleber´. In Saulgau, Kleber not only welcomed every express train at the station, he also had specialties from Munich brought to his hotel by train. But since the late 1970s, there were plans to shut down the Herbertingen-Kißlegg railway line, on which Saulgau is located, due to growing DB deficits. With a good connection to the DB management and a lot of commitment, Kleber always managed to save his train. After all, this was even officially listed in the timetable as 'Kleber-Express'. But in 2000, Kleber had to give up his hotel due to payment difficulties. And in 2003 the Kleber-Express was discontinued. Kleber later ran a hotel in Bad Herrenalb near Karlsruhe. One thing that should have made it easier for railway enthusiast Kleber: the hotel has its own mountain railway.

Leutkirch's citizen´s station (Bürgerbahnhof)

Leutkirch station

In April 2012, the Leutkirch station was opened to the public after a renovation as a citizens' station. In recognition of this event, the Baden-Württemberg Monument Foundation named the station (built in 1889) Monument of the Month. More than two million euros were invested in the renovation of the station, a good half of which was raised through civic involvement. The city, which had taken over the station from the railway company for 230,000 euros in 1998, was not able to cover the renovation costs on its own. However, Christian Skrodzki, a committed citizen of Leutkirch, recognized the architectural value of the station and founded a cooperative to collect money for reconstruction and renovation. He hoped that the people of Leutkirch would be persuaded to subscribe to 1000 shares at 1000 euros each to raise one million euros. The shares sold faster than expected, however, and eventually, they even had to issue 111 more shares to meet the demand. Soon, television crews and ministers appeared in the station, and the project received several awards.

16. Bayern (Bavaria)

16.1 Mittelfranken/Middle Franconia

Nuremberg main station and the monument

Nuremberg was the first German city with railroad traffic (the Nuremberg-Fürth line was opened in 1835). The city was also on the first state-owned Bavarian long-distance line: the Ludwigsbahn from Hof to Lindau. However, Nuremberg did not have a representative station for a long time. The mayor Schuh, therefore, spoke to the Prince Regent Luitpold of Bavaria (1821-1912), and said, "Your Royal Highness, we have now built a monument to you, for which we would simply need a new station." Subsequently, the project was approved. Originally, the architecture of the station was rejected by the general public because instead of a sandstone façade, as is usual in Nuremberg, it has a shell limestone façade and the neo-renaissance style was not everyone's cup of tea.

When Nuremberg became the 'City of the Reich Party Congresses' in the Third Reich, the Nazis melted down the station's equestrian figure of Prince Regent Luitpold. In its place is an advertising column in front of the station entrance, which can still be seen there today and now looks old-fashioned. Under the station, there is a bunker, which saved the lives of many Nuremberg citizens during the Second World War. The bunker's flue is hidden in the advertising pillar.

Fürth´s Ludwigsbahnhof

Besides Nuremberg, Fürth was the first German city with a railway station in 1835. Between 1885 and 1886, the modest building of the Ludwigsbahnhof was replaced by a more representative station. This station, named after the Ludwigseisenbahn, was demolished by the Nazis in 1938 to make room for a deployment area, which was also to have military-strategic significance (space for air defence guns). On the occasion of the 175th anniversary of the railway in 2010, the station was rebuilt as a model (tarpaulins printed with the station facade on a scaffolding) on a scale of 1: 1.5 on the Fürther Freiheit (a local market and event square). The mockup was dismantled after only two weeks.

Left and right of the Pegnitz

There are two parallel railway lines from Nuremberg to the east. The line to the left (south) of the Pegnitz was opened in 1859 by the private Bavarian East Railway as a connection between Nuremberg and Regensburg via Amberg. The state railway line on the right of the Pegnitz established the connection to Bayreuth from 1877. Places like Lauf and Hersbruck thus received stations on the left and right of the river. The stations of the Ostbahn (East Line) had gabled roofs and two stories, while the stations on the right of the Pegnitz (built 20 years later by the Staatsbahn) had flat hip roofs, sandstone facades, and three stories. The middle floors of the buildings on the right side of the river have smaller windows; these were intended as an apartment for station servants and helpers. Behind the larger windows, the stationmaster lived on the top floor. Stations such as those of Pegnitz and Rupprechtstegen still show this today.

Erlangen customs house and the manatee

A 'secondary line' (branch line) connected Erlangen with Neunkirchen am Brand until 1963. This railway line was also called Seku or Seacow in the local vernacular. There is an anecdote about the origin of this nickname: there was once a station restaurant at the inner-city stop Erlangen-Zollhaus. A painter did not appreciate the inscription "Sekundärbahn (Secondary Line)" above the station. Therefore, over the weekend, he replaced it with the inscription "Restaurant for the Seku." Students who passed by promptly gave the railway the nickname Seekuh (Manatee).

The cabaret artist and the main station

Klaus Karl-Kraus (*1951), a cabaret artist from Erlangen, was annoyed that his hometown did not have a central railway station. After each performance, he collected signatures for the renaming of the local station and sent them to the then-head of the railway company Hartmut Mehdorn at the end of 2005. On 14 December 2005, Kraus announced that Mehdorn (1999-2009 Chairman of the Board of Management of DB AG) had taken good note of the letter and promised to add the word "Haupt (Central)" to the station's title. The prospect of the station's name actually being changed was perceived by locals as being too optimistic since the railway did not do anything to rename the station. However, the bus stop at the station is now called Hauptbahnhof (central station) by the transport companies of the Nuremberg area.

Treuchtlingen and the bomb hit

In the underpass of Treuchtlingen station, a marble plaque commemorates one of the greatest war tragedies of the railway. On 23 February 1945, when a train carrying troops on holiday from the front stopped at the station, the Allies launched an air raid. The passengers fled into the platform underpass. However, that is where a bomb hit. Three hundred people died in the underpass, and almost six hundred additionally perished inside the station and its surrounding areas. When the wooden cross on the roof of St. Mary's Church, built in 1934 and located not far from the station, was removed in the early 1990s to be replaced by a new one, the old cross was still peppered with bomb splinters and bullets.

16.2 Oberfranken/Upper Franconia

Hof - the divided station

In 1880, the terminus station in the centre of Hof, which had become too small, was replaced by a through station. The entrance hall of the old railway station, built in 1848 in the style of a three-nave basilica, is (shortened) still preserved today. The new station was symmetrically laid out with a Saxon part in the north and a Bavarian part in the south because Hof was the border station of the kingdoms Saxony and Bavaria. In the middle of the station building, a magnificent royal hall was created for a meeting of the representatives of both countries. However, the kings of Bavaria and Saxony never met here. Later, this part of the building was used as a station restaurant. Today, there is also a railway station bookstore here. The station building is over 137 metres wide on the trackside and thus, as the rather Protestant Hofer emphasise, only three metres shorter than the façade of St. Peter's Cathedral in Rome. By the way, the Vatican also has a railway station, although it is considerably smaller than Hof's building.

The refugee train

On 30 September 1989, a special, very full train arrived at Hof central station carrying refugees of the GDR. In the late summer of '89, several GDR citizens fled the country and went to the BDR embassy in Prague. Finally, the then-GDR head of state Erich Honecker released the embassy refugees, who were allowed to leave by train for the West. As the GDR state's last demonstration of power, however, he pushed through the decision that the train should first pass through GDR territory. In Dresden, three young people succeeded in jumping on the train. Later on the trip, in Plauen, the citizens cheered the train, although this was forbidden. Finally, the first station in the west, Hof, was reached. Including subsequent trains, a total of 13600 people arrived here. Today, a monument on the south side of the station commemorates the events in autumn 1989.

Lichtenfels - the basket city

Lichtenfels, today a regional railway junction in northern Bavaria, was connected to the Ludwig Nord-Südbahn (Bavaria's first state railway) as early as 1846. The station building, also built in 1846 according to plans of the Gärtner school, is one of the oldest in Bavaria. Flowers are displayed in a basket in front of the station in summer because Lichtenfels is known as the basket city and was once (together with Michelau) an important centre of basket weaving.

Not far from Lichtenfels is the Franconian Forest. It was once said that "Amsterdam is built on the Franconian Forest" because, in the 19th century, tree trunks from the Franconian Forest were brought by raft over the Main and Rhine to Holland, where they were used in shipbuilding and also in town planning. Thus, the Amsterdam main railway station rests on thousands of tree trunks from the Franconian Forest.

Neuenmarkt-Wirsberg and the inclined plane

The radio station "Antenne Bayern" has a list of "100 places in Bavaria that you must see in your life." The only railway-related sight on the list is Neuenmarkt-Wirsberg, which is labeled the "craziest railway station in Bavaria." In 1848, the so-called inclined plane between this station and Markt-schorgast was put into operation, where - over a very short distance - steam locomotives overcame 148 meters of altitude change. Additionally, many different locomotives were stationed here. Antenne Bayern thinks more steam locomotives are stationed here than in any other place in Germany.

Rothenbürg and the mix-up

Rothenbürg is a district of the city of Selbitz in the Upper Franconian district of Hof. Here, there is a small train stop on the Hof-Bad Steben line, a pub, but no hotel.

Although Rothenbürg actually has no sights, 250 to 300 tourists, who believe they are in the tourist hotspot Rothenburg ob der Tauber, arrive here every year. Therefore, the railway company Agilis, which serves the line, has developed leaflets - with hints in English, French, Italian, Chinese, Korean, and Japanese - describing how to get from Rothenbürg to Rothenburg ob der Tauber. The trek is possible via Nuremberg but involves several transfers and takes approximately 3.5 hours. The English version of the pamphlet is quite poorly translated and reads, "You are now her, but you want here. Sorry to inform you, that you sit in the wrong train."

It is not known how many of these tourists find the not so easy way by train to Rothenburg ob der Tauber.

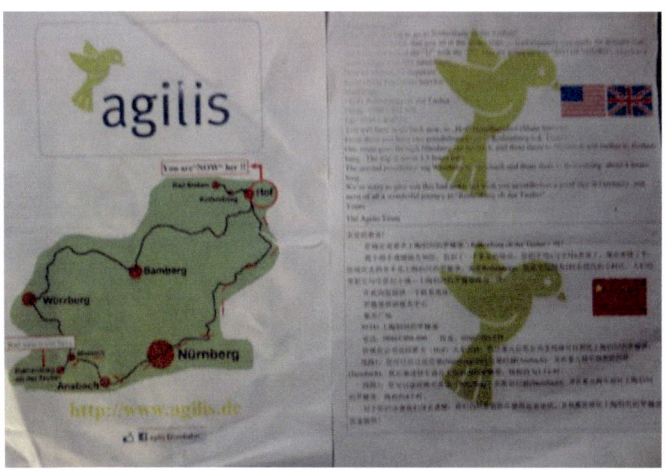

Flyer distributed by railway company Agilis to tourists

Würzburg central station and the investment backlog

On February 23, 1945, the second railway station of Würzburg (built by Friedrich Bürklein in 1869) was largely destroyed in an air raid that had actually been directed at Bayreuth. Between 1953 and 1954, a new station in the modern style was built. The northern side wall was decorated with the painting of a steam locomotive. As parts of the wall covering came loose, the painting was dismantled and installed in the transport museum in Nuremberg. Because the station was becoming in need of renovation, the newspaper *Bild am Sonntag* awarded it the title "Ugliest station in Germany" in 2005. A project to modernise the station as part of the construction of a shopping centre failed in 2006 due to a citizens' decision. Improvements are now being made, and the elegant 1950s building is becoming ever more beautiful and functional.

Aschaffenburg and the messenger of the gods

In 2009, the 1950s station building of Aschaffenburg was demolished to make way for a new building, which was inaugurated at the beginning of 2011. Local architecture experts protested against the demolition, as the Aschaffenburg station was considered one of the most beautiful station buildings in Germany at the time of its construction. Nevertheless, thanks to an action by the artist Udo Breitenbach, the *Messenger of the Gods*—a ceramic façade decoration showing Hermes with two suitcases—was at least partially saved. Because the cost of 20,000 euros for professional dismantling was too high for the city councils, Breitenbach tried to do the work himself with scaffolding, flex, and hammer. Due to the danger of collapse, Breitenbach's work had to be stopped before Hermes' scarf and the 'winged wheel' could be salvaged.

Erbendorf against Erbendorf

Erbendorf, a small town (5300 inhabitants) located in the Upper Palatinate at the southern Steinwald, does not have a railway connection anymore, and yet, the town has an interesting railway history. In the 1860s, when the Bavarian East Railways planned a railway line to Bohemia, there were considerations to make Erbendorf a hub. However, Weiden was chosen for this role. Twenty years later, another opportunity for the town was missed. When a shorter connection was planned from Weiden to Marktredwitz, the track could have gone via Erbendorf. Yet, the town failed to submit a petition, and the route went via Wiesau and Pechbrunn. It was not until 1909 that Erbendorf was connected to the railway network via a 6.5 km long local railway. However, the town could not agree on the station's location. The people of North Erbendorf argued with the people of South Erbendorf about the location. There was a stalemate in the local council because there were as many 'northerners' as 'southerners' represented. The dispute went so far that in school, a child from Nord-Erbendorf was no longer allowed to sit next to a child from Süd-Erbendorf. Even the French daily newspaper *Le Temps* reported on the station dispute under the headline "Erbendorf in Bavaria: A Model and Example of German Unity." In the end, one station was built in Erbendorf-South and another in Erbendorf-North. To finance a second station, the entire community forest was cleared. However, the stations had a shorter life span than most trees. Passenger traffic on the line was closed down as early as 1972, and in 1997, freight traffic was also shut down.

The moved station of Pechbrunn

While Erbendorf was struggling to get two stations, the village of Groschlattengrün on the Ostbahn did not want a station at all. The railway engineers visited the village because a junction station was needed on the single-track Ostbahn, and the village was located almost exactly in between the stations of Wiesau and Marktredwitz. However, the Groschlatten-Grüners managed to locate the station in the nearby district of Pechbrunn, which consisted of only a few houses. Nevertheless, the station was given the name Groschlattengrün. In 1900, the railway facilities had to be extended, yet, the area was enclosed by the station and a ballast works. Therefore, a new station foundation was built 10 m away from it, the station was separated from the ground, and the building was moved centimetre by centimetre to its new location using rollers and cable winches. Meanwhile, normal service continued inside. Back then, this was a major event, and special trains brought onlookers from Hof, Bayreuth, and Eger.

Neukirchen and Karl Marx

Since 1875, there was a railway connection from Neukirchen - located near Sulzbach-Rosenberg on the eastern railway line - to Weiden in the Upper Palatinate. In 1973, this line was extended to a main line.

In August 1876, however, Karl Marx (1818-1883), who was on his way to Karlsbad for a cure, missed his connection in Neukirchen due to an unreliable train conductor. At the station of Irrenlohe (near Schwandorf), he could not find a connecting train to the Northern Upper Palatinate, so he had to return to Neukirchen. Therefore, the station had the honour of welcoming the important economist and social theorist twice in one day.

Regenstauf and Thomas Mann

In 1894, the writer Thomas Mann (1875-1955), born in Lübeck, moved to Munich to live with his mother and siblings. On May 1, 1906, he travelled from Munich to Dresden in a 1st class sleeping car compartment. At 21:30, not long after the train had left Regensburg, a train accident occurred not far from the Regenstauf station. Mann described the accident in his novella *Das Eisenbahnunglück* (The Railway Accident) from 1908:

"We were close to a small station, not far from Regensburg. The big express train was broken in two. The cause for the accident: a defective switch."

From Regensburg and Schwandorf, rescue trains soon arrived at the scene of the accident. Mann got as far as Hof, from where he could continue his journey to Dresden. Since 1999, a memorial plaque at the Regenstaufen railway underpass has been commemorating the railway accident, which has gone down in literary history, although relatively lightly.

Regensburg

The city of Regensburg escaped the Second World War with little damage. However, the station was considerably damaged by bombs due to its hub function. It was rebuilt in a simple style in 1955. The Regensburg-Arcaden shopping centre was built south of the station in 2004. The shopping centre was connected to the station by a light, modern arcade walkway. At the same time, the dingy railway underpass was closed down. The aim of the closure was to make a good impression since the city was a UNESCO World Heritage candidate. However, the old underpass was not filled up since it could still be used for emergencies. Yet, it is now in such a state that hardly anyone would enter it voluntarily.

16.5 Oberbayern/Upper Bavaria

Munich's first train station

In 1839, Munich got its first railway station: a wooden building of the private Munich-Augsburg railway. It does not seem to have been particularly representative. In a rhyme of a station warden, passed down through the generation, it was called a shack.

Munich Main Station and the gas explosion

In 1847, Munich's first station burned down after only eight years of existence. The Franconian Friedrich Bürklein, the architect of the Augsburg Central Station, designed the second Munich Station, which was completed in 1849. It had a church-like appearance and was considered the "Basilica of Transport." Until the 1920s, further buildings were added, the station front was extended, and the Starnberg and Holzkirchner stations were added to the side wings. Thus, the station finally lacked the closed and monument-like appearance of other big city stations. Hitler, therefore, wanted to replace it with a gigantic through station, which would have a large dome, further west, but the plans were never implemented. During the Second World War, over 60% of the station was destroyed, and in 1960, a rather banal new building was opened. Reconstruction measures in the 1980s added glazed shop fronts and a gallery on a second level. The press commented that the overall structure gave the impression that a gas explosion had taken place. Finally a new station building with offices is now under construction, but it will still take years until it is completed.

Munich-Pasing, old station

Munich is not exactly rich in historical railway station architecture. The previously mentioned central station is not particularly attractive from an architectonic point of view, the Ostbahnhof is considered an architectural void, and most of the S-Bahn stations are sober functional buildings. Therefore, it is surprising that an old, well-preserved, and architecturally historically important Munich station building was almost forgotten and left to decay. This is the old station in Munich-Pasing, which was opened in 1848 and had fallen into disrepair due to a new station building, located 70 m to the west and built by Georg Friedrich Seidel in 1873. However, during the construction of the Pasing Arcaden shopping centre, the building was renovated in 2010-2011 and converted into a restaurant, which is currently called Alex. The name fit because Alex is also the abbreviation of the Allgäu-Express, which stops in Pasing.

Munich-Isartalbahnhof and the Jerusalemexpress

In Geretsried, south of Munich, there were armament factories before the Second World War. For employees and workers of these factories, the settlement Föhrenwald was built in 1939, which could house more than 4000 inhabitants. After the end of the war, the undestroyed settlement was set up by the Allies as temporary accommodation for Jewish survivors. Soon after, a separate Jewish world of life, with 6000 inhabitants, was created here, shielded away from the Bavarian environment. Since the trains of the Isartalbahn Wolfratshausen-Munich line (where the Isartalbahnhof Thalkirchen was the terminus) were heavily used by the Jewish refugees, it was soon referred to as the "Jerusalem Express" in the local vernacular.

Munich Stachus

Munich's Karlsplatz - called Stachus by locals due to a pub that was located there - is currently an important local traffic junction with tram, underground, and suburban railway. At the square, a stranger once asked the actor Karl Valentin, "How far is it from here to the central station?" Valentin replied, "If you go on like this, it's 40,000 kilometres. Yet, if you turn around, it's only five minutes."

The Deisenhofen station bar and the Radler beer

Deisenhofen is a suburban railway station south of Munich on the line to Holzkirchen. The Deisenhofen station restaurant once played a certain role in the invention of Radler Beer (Shandy): a mixture of beer and lemonade. Franz Xaver Kugler is considered the inventor of the Radler beer. Kugler was originally a track construction worker on the Munich-Holzkirchen line, which was extended to two tracks at the end of the 19th century. Since the work was hard and the next inn was far away, Kugler took over the supply of beer to his colleagues. He fetched the beer from the Deisenhofen station tavern and brought it to the construction site by horse and cart. Yet, that was too complicated in the long run. Therefore, Kugler set up a booth at the construction site, which under the name "Kantine der Königlich-Bayerischen Eisenbahn zu Deisenhofen (Royal Bavarian Railway Canteen at Deisenhofen)" took over the supply of the construction workers. After the completion of the railway line, it became the Waldrestaurant in 1897, and later, a stately restaurant, the Kugler-Alm, which developed into a popular place for excursions. When the bicycle became increasingly popular in the 1920s, Kugler had a cycle path built right through the forest. This excursion route, which is still popular today, was enthusiastically received by the people of Munich. On a beautiful Saturday in summer 1922, 13,000 cyclists are said to have stormed the Kugler Alm. However, the beer supply could not withstand this thirst. Kugler found a way out to fulfill the demand: he mixed half of the beer (which was running low) with lemonade (which was still in plentiful supply) and served this to the guests. He stated that he had invented this drink particularly for cyclists so that they did not have to ride their bikes home swaying.

The blue Uffing railway station

The station at Uffing am Staffelsee was one of the first Plus Energie stations in Germany. The Finkbeiner family, the founders of the station, financed an energetic renovation, installed a wood facade, and installed a photovoltaic system on the roof. The station building thus generates more energy than it consumes. A battery system with 24 modules stores the generated electricity so that e-bikes and electric cars can be charged via two charging stations. The station is also home to the German children and youth foundation Plant-for-the-Planet, which aims to plant trees for a better world.

Geltendorf's colourful S-Bahn

On the morning of 26 March 1985, a Bavarian train driver made an astonishing discovery. For the first time in Germany, an entire S-Bahn train - which had been parked overnight in Geltendorf - had been sprayed with graffiti. Graffiti had spread in New York in the seventies, where the spray pioneers had sprayed 200 subway cars. In the early eighties, the spray reached the first big-city trains in Europe. Among the sprayers from Geltendorf was Loomit (born in Celle in 1968), who made his debut in 1983 with a graffiti on the Buchloe water tower. The spray pioneers later switched to the art establishment (today graffiti costs the railways 40 million a year and is considered more like vandalism). Loomit entered the Guinness Book of Records in 1995 with the highest graffiti in the world, and in 2002, he was awarded the Schwabing Art Prize by Munich's mayor Christian Ude.

The train without an engine driver

Locomotive drivers have to be very disciplined and are actually not allowed to drink too much because there are no toilets on locomotives. That was also the reason why a driver of a Munich S-Bahn was in a great hurry and left his train at the Ebersberg terminus on 31 December 1988. However, he forgot to adjust the brakes. When he returned, he got a slight shock: the S-Bahn had disappeared. Between Ebersberg and the Inn valley, there is a slight gradient, and the low rolling friction steel wheel rail caused the train to roll, driven only by gravity, to set itself in motion. The train only came to a stop 19 kilometers later at Wasserburg station (which is 100 meters lower in altitude than Ebersberg).

Grafrath and the Moss Cow

The western shore of the Ammersee could only be reached by rail after the completion of the Ammersee railway in 1898. Five years later, the eastern shore of the lake was also connected by rail after the completion of the railway line to Herrsching. Before that, one had to get off at Grafrath station (Munich-Lindau railway line), walk to the Amper river, and then take a steamship - which had been running to Lake Ammersee since 1880 - from there. Since the Amper led through swampy terrain, this ship was popularly called Mooskuh (moss cow). To serve the thirsty excursionists, a "Wirtshaus zum Dampfschiff (Tavern of the Steamship)" soon opened at the landing stage in Grafrath, which existed until 1939.

Klais - formerly the highest intercity railway station

On the scenic route Garmisch-Mittenwald-Innsbruck, lies the small railway station Klais. The station is so proud of its record that the Bavarian Alpine style station building was given the inscription "Germany's highest intercity station,

933 m." However, since the timetable change in December 2007, no Intercity stops here anymore. Nevertheless, the inscription at the station remains. After all, there have been ICE test runs on the line since then.

Bad Reichenhall and the 'three brothers

Just before the end of WWII in Europe, on April 25, 1945, an air raid, in which 198 people died, was launched on the Upper Bavarian spa town of Bad Reichenhall (today also popularly nicknamed 'Bad Leichenhall [Morturary]' because of the many people who had moved to the town to rest). The railway station, a Bürklein building, was also destroyed. In 1952, the architect Karl Fackler designed a new building in the simple, functional style of the time, which was opened in 1955. Fackler had opened similar station buildings for Traunstein (opened in 1954) and Freilassing (1955). Therefore, the three station buildings are collectively called "three brothers."

Landsberg - the citizen station

Today, Landsberg am Lech is only connected to the railway network by a short spur line. However, due to commuters to Munich and Augsburg, the number of passengers is not insignificant. With the support of the city and the district, Ideal Mobil AG (a Munich mobility service provider) acquired the Landsberg train station from DB in 2005 and converted it into a Bürgerbahnhof (citizen station): a modern mobility centre with various service facilities (see www.bahnhof-landsberg.de). In 2006, this project was awarded the Bavarian public transport prize, and now, a similar project is being promoted in Füssen with its modest station building, yet, no real progress has been made so far. Further projects include the Bürgerbahnhof in Murnau and Leutkirch in Württemberg.

St. Ottilien and the flowers

The monastery railway station of St. Ottilien, situated on the Ammerseebahn, has already been described by the press and television (pictures of a Bavarian Radio programme are posted at the station) as "Germany's most beautiful railway station." The music group *Jodelwahnsinn* also recorded a CD with the railway station scenery as background.

The first station building from 1898 was a small corrugated iron hut. The current station building was built in 1938 in the local style, and its front side is decorated with a Lüftlmalerei (Art Gallery) Additionally, the station has displayed lovingly tended and almost opulent floral decoration.

St. Ottilien Station

This was thanks to the stationmaster Elisabeth Polke (*1929), who managed the station from 1958 to 2002. Since Mrs. Polke is retired in a house only a few metres from the station building and tends to her flowery garden, which directly borders on the platform, passengers still do not have to live without flower arrangements at the station. The station building itself has now been bought by the nearby monastery, whose name it bears, and rented out to a photo studio.

Possenhofen and Sisi

The railway station of Possenhofen at the Starnberger See is also called Kaiserin Sisi-Bahnhof. The station was built by the Neuschwanstein architect Georg v. Dollmann. Not far from the station is the castle Possenhofen. Duchess Elisabeth, called "Sisi," was Empress of Austria by marriage from 1854 until 1898 and stayed there at Possenhofen often. Accordingly, the nearby station was equipped with a noble waiting room in the style of late classicism. In November 2004, the station building was bought by a group of private investors. In 2008, it was renovated, and an Empress Elisabeth Museum was established in it. The municipality was approached with the request to officially name the nameless station forecourt Empress Elisabeth Platz. However, the square still has no name.

16.6 Niederbayern/Lower Bavaria

The station without rails

At the end of the 19th century, the village of Wittibreut in Lower Bavaria could not have expected to be connected to the railway network. A farmer from Wittibreut, therefore, built a railway station in 1876, although it was uncertain whether the village would get a rail connection since the route Simbach/Inn - Vilshofen had not yet been confirmed. The railway station was also built on a hill, whereas railway lines tend to run in valleys. Eventually, Wittibreut was not connected to the railway network, and the station remained without rails. Yet, the building is now a historically protected.

Bayerisch Eisenstein and the Iron Curtain

The train station of Bayerisch Eisenstein in the Bavarian Forest is located on the border to the Czech Republic. Due to a state treaty between Austria and Bavaria in 1851, the Bayerische Ostbahn and a Bohemian railway company built the sections of the line on their respective sides of the border leading to this border town. The central section of the reception hall, completed in 1878, was placed exactly on the border and designed to be very representative. In the waiting room, the large "Cologne ceiling," a special ceiling construction with beams and stucco, is still preserved. The railway line was intended to be the shortest connection between Munich and Prague, yet, it never saw much traffic due to the topographically unfavourable route. At the time of the Iron Curtain, traffic came to a complete standstill as the tracks were interrupted by a fence. Yet, in 1991, the border crossing was reopened, and one could change to the trains of the Czech State Railways CD. Since May 2006, Bavarian trains have even been driving seven km across the border to the Czech town of Picak, where you can continue by train to Prague or reach winter sports areas.

Klingenbrunn - Germany's coldest railway station?

In the Spiegelau district of Klingenbrunn station, not far from the train station, there is an official weather measuring station. This measuring station records the coldest temperatures of the Bavarian Forest, which is not exactly spoiled by warmth. Sometimes, Klingenbrunn station is also called the coldest place in Germany. Therefore, Klingenbrunn Station (the station building is now used by private individuals as their home) may be the coldest DB station in Germany on an annual average.

Passau and the murdered police officers

Once, the main station of Passau was used by the Austrian ÖBB as well as by the DB as a railway station for inland traffic. Therefore, there were two passenger underpasses, separated by a wall. After Austria joined the EU in 1995, the walls were demolished. However, one piece of the wall was left, and a memorial plaque was placed there. This commemorates the policemen Klaus März and Georg Schachner, who were shot dead by a Serbian arms smuggler in November 1993 at passport control in the Intercity Donaukurier between Linz and Passau.

In Passau, Germany's first 'bridge post office' was set up in 1975 on a footbridge over the tracks.

Straubing and the mix-up

The relatively small Neufahrn has an almost oversized station building (built in 1873), while the larger city of Straubing has a modest station. Therefore, some believe that the construction plans were once mixed up.

Augsburg Central Station - the mobility hub

Augsburg's central station, built in 1846 by Friedrich Bürklein, is the oldest still in operation in a major German city. It was also the first station with a passenger tunnel. A tram tunnel with an underground stop is now under construction, and the main station is to be developed into a 'mobility hub' by 2022.

☞ *Allegedly, Bertold Brecht, born in Augsburg, said that "the best thing about Augsburg is the fast train to Munich."*

Schmiechen (Swabia)

From the Swabian district capital Augsburg, one can take the Ammersee railway to Schmiechen, which has been part of Swabia since the regional reform (in the 1970s). However, Schmiechen's station sign still bears the words "Upper Bavaria" today. After the mistake was recognized, no one in the community - which actually felt that it belonged to Upper Bavaria - wanted to raise the funds required by the railway for the renaming.

Lindau - the railway that fell into the water

In 1905, two freight cars broke away from a locomotive in Oberstaufen in the Allgäu region and rolled 53 km in length and 400 metres in altitude downhill to Lindau, where they crashed into Lake Constance. Although Lindau is considered a terminus station, some freight tracks run past the side of the reception hall and once led across the pier almost up to the lighthouse. From there, they went directly to the ships, on which tracks were also laid, because Lindau was once an important ferry port for goods traffic to and from Switzerland. Grain from Hungary and Romania arrived here and was brought to Switzerland in wagons on ships. In the opposite direction, even oranges from Spain came across

Lake Constance. In 1937, 100 freight cars were still being transported every day.

The Somali railway station

In Somalia, which was devastated by civil war, there is no rail transport and no functioning railway station today. Nevertheless, there was a "Somaliabahnhof" until 2017 in Gersthofen, Swabia. The graffiti-covered station building, with its covered or broken windows, reminded the local population of a scene from the country embroiled in a civil war. Ironically, the "most rotten station in Bavaria" was also called the "jewel of Swabia." The city finally bought the building and had it demolished in 2017.

Hindelang and the hunting ground

If the people of Hindelang want to travel by train, they have to go to Sonthofen because the village is not located on a railway line. Yet, in Hindelang, there is a cube-shaped building that was once planned as a railway station. However, the Bavarian Prince Regent Luitpold had a hunting ground nearby and decided that he "did not want a train," because, "it whistles and drives away the deer."

Wasserburg and Martin Walser

The writer Martin Walser was born on 27 March 1927 in Wasserburg on Lake Constance. His parental home was opposite the Wasserburg railway station, and his parents ran the local station restaurant. Walser went to grammar school in Lindau and still lives on Lake Constance in the Überlingen district of Nußdorf. There is also a train stop in Nußdorf, where Walser's daughter, Johanna, picks up journalists.

Memmingen and the only modular station

In 2001, a modern reception hall was put into operation in Memmingen station. With the functional new building, a modular concept was introduced that was to be used for new buildings throughout Germany. However, the station building became more expensive than planned. Instead of becoming a model for other stations, it remained the only modular DB building.

Legau and the return ticket

At the end of the 1960s, a bus station was established at the Memmingen railway station. When the branch line to Legau was shut down in 1972, a corresponding stub track was removed, and the bus station widened. Therefore, the following story would now no longer possible.

Once, a farmer was on his way to Legau by train. When the conductor arrived, a priest was sitting in the compartment. The farmer could not find his ticket and started cursing. He said, "Where the hell is the ticket for the sacrament of harlots?" The priest replied, "If you continue to curse like that, then don't come to Legau, or you'll go straight to hell." In response, the Swabian farmer said, "I don't mind because it's a return ticket."

Annex

1.   List of station nicknames

a) Berlin

Hauptbahnhof	Kathedrale des Reisens
Hauptbahnhof	Glaspalast mit Wüste
Ostkreuz	Rostkreuz

Former nicknames

Anhalter Bhf	Mutterhöhle der Eisenbahn
Anhalter Bhf	Tor in die Blaue Ferne
Lehrter Bhf	Schloss unter den Bahnhöfen
Friedrichstraße	Tränenpalast (Grenzübergangsstelle)
Schlesischer Bhf	Katholischer Bahnhof
Zoologischer Garten	Heimlicher Hauptbahnhof
	Urologischer Garten

b) Rest of Germany

Altenbeken Bhf	Fünffingerbahnhof
Bad Liebenzell Bhf	Marmorbahnhof
Cuxhaven-Amerika Bhf	once: Bahnhof der Tränen
Dortmund Hbf	Pommesbude mit Gleisanschluss
Gersthofen	Somaliabahnhof
Hamburg-Altona	Kaufhaus mit Gleisanschluss
Hamburg Dammtor	once: Kaiserbahnhof
Hannover Nordstadt	Blaue Grotte
Kassel-Wilhelmshöhe	Palast der tausend Winde
Kassel-Wilhemshöhe	Größte Tankstelle der Welt (Vordach)
Köln Hbf	Bahnhofskapelle
Leipzig Hbf	Einkaufszentrum mit Gleisanschluss
Leverkusen-Mitte	Bahnhofs-Klo
Ludwigshafen Hbf	once: Modernster Bahnhof Europas
Mechernich Bhf	Miniaturbahnhof
Oldenburg	Klinkerburg
Solingen Hbf	once: Gammelbahnhof
Uelzen	Hundertwasserbahnhof
Unterneudorf/Sachsen	Stachelbeerbahnhof (Haltepunkt)

2. Stations, that got an award

a) Designated by *Allianz pro Schiene* (Berlin) as *Railway Station of the Year (Bahnhof des Jahres)*

	City station	Small town station
2004	Hannover Hbf	Lübben Bhf
2005	Mannheim Hbf	Weimar Hbf
2006	Hamburg Dammtor	Oberstdorf
2007	Berlin Hbf	Landsberg/Lech
2008	Karlsruhe Hbf	Schwerin Hbf
2009	Erfurt Hbf	Uelzen
2010	Darmstadt Hbf	Baden-Baden
2011	Leipzig Hbf	Halberstadt Hbf
2012	Bremen Hbf	Aschaffenburg Hbf
2013	Göttingen Hbf	Oberursel
2014	Dresden Hbf	Hünfeld

(from 2015 no split between city/small town)

2015	Marburg	Obstfelderschmiede
2016	Stralsund	Steinheim (Westfalen)
2017	Lutherstadt Wittenb.	Bayerisch Eisenstein
2018	Winterberg	Eppstein
2019	Cuxhaven	Bad Bentheim
2020	Altötting	Rottenbach (Königsee)

Source: www.allianz-pro-schiene.de

b) European Route of Industrial Heritage

Country	Station
Germany	Dresden Hbf

UK: London St. Pancras Station, Spain: Madrid Atocha
Quelle: http://de.erih.net

c) Renault Traffic Award

Year	Station
2001	Station tunnel Henningsdorf
2002	Airport Hannover Lichtbahnhof
2003	Long distance station Airport Rhein-Main, Recognition: Bhf Oberstdorf, Hbf Mainz
2004	Haltepunkt Ludwigshafen Mitte
2006	Berlin Hbf

http://www.renault-traffic-design.de

d) European Rail Award

2013	Small station: Eschwege
2014	Small station: Melsungen

3. Important railway station architects

Architect	Stations
Friedrich Eisenlohr (*Lörrach, 1805-1854)	Lahr, Emmendingen und Denzlingen. First stations of Mannheim, Karlsruhe, Freiburg, Heidelberg. Style: neo-gothic
Friedrich Bürklein (1813-1872)	Augsburg Hbf, Bamberg, old stations of Munich und Würzburg
Fritz Klingholz (* Wuppertal 1861-1921)	Koblenz Hbf (1899-1902) Lübeck Hbf (1908), Lübeck-Travemünde (1913) Worms Hbf (1904), Wiesbaden Hbf (1904-1906)
Paul Bonatz (1877-1956)	Stuttgart Hbf (1914-1927) Style: neue Sachlichkeit
Meinard von Gerkan (*Riga, 1935)	Berlin Hauptbahnhof (2006) Style: Modern glass architecture

4. The largest German stations according to the number of passengers and visitors, working days

Railway total: 11 million /day

Land	Travellers and visitors/day (x1000)
Baden-Württemberg	Stuttgart Hbf 300, Mannheim Hbf 100, Freiburg 60, Karlsruhe Hbf 60, Pforzheim 50, Tübingen 50, Heidelberg 30, Ulm 29,
Bavaria (Bayern)	München Hbf 400, München-Pasing 85, Nürnberg 200, Augsburg 44, Würzburg 34, Bamberg 15, Aschaffenburg 14, Oberstdorf 1.5
Berlin	Hauptbahnhof 300, Friedrichstraße 220, Alexanderplatz 150, Gesundbrunnen 140, Südkreuz 110, Zoo 100, Ostbahnhof 100, Lichtenberg 85, Potsdamer P. 50, Spandau 50
Bremen	Hauptbahnhof 120, Bremerhaven < 10
Brandenburg	Potsdam 50, Cottbus 12, Frankfurt/O 13
Hamburg	Hauptbahnhof 550, Altona 100, Harburg 45, Dammtor 43, Bergedorf 35
Hesse (Hessen)	Frankfurt Hbf 460, Wiesbaden 41, Darmstadt 40, , Fulda 20, Gießen 20, Kassel-Wilh.16, Kassel Hbf 12, Limburg-Süd 3
Mecklenburg.-V	Rostock 33, Schwerin 12, Stralsund 10
Lower Saxony (Niedersachsen)	Hannover Hbf 280, Braunschweig 80, Hildesheim 31, Göttingen 28, Osnabrück 25, Oldenburg 25, Wolfsburg 7
NRW	Köln Hbf 310, Düsseldorf Hbf 270, Essen Hbf 150, Duisburg 130, Dortmund 110, Münster 65, Bonn 67, Bochum 65, Bielefeld 40, Wuppertal 40, Aachen 25, Gelsenk. 18, Hagen 30
Rhineland-Palat. (Rheinland-Pfalz)	Mainz Hbf 55, Koblenz Hbf 40, Ludwigshafen Hbf 10-20, Montabaur 2
Saarland	Saarbrücken Hbf 27, Dillingen 0.6
Sachsen	Leipzig 120, Dresden: Hbf 60, Neustadt 30; Chemnitz 30
Sachsen-Anhalt	Magdeburg 40, Halle 30, Bitterfeld 6
Schleswig- Hols.	Lübeck Hbf 31, Kiel 25, Niebüll 3.5
Thuringia (Thüringen)	Erfurt Hbf 34, Weimar 14, Gera 9 Jena West 5, Naumburg 3, Ilmenau 1

Quelle: DB, Wikipedia, verschiedene Webseiten zur Bahn

Literature

Bund Deutscher Architekten (Hrsg.)
Renaissance der Bahnhöfe
Vieweg Verlag, Braunschweig 1996

Deutsche Bundesbahn (Hrsg.)
65 Jahre Stuttgarter Hauptbahnhof 1922-1987
Stuttgart 1987

Walter Engels, Günter Klotz, Jochen Lengermann
Mitten in Deutschland – Bahnhof Kassel-Wilhelmshöhe
Hestra- Verlag, Darmstadt 1991

Roland Feitenhansl
Der Bahnhof Heilbronn
DGEG Medien, Hövelhof 2003

Helmut Frei
Bahnhofsguide Deutschland 1995/96
Verlag Stadler, Konstanz 1995

Helmut Freitag
Bahn&City, Bahnhofsguide Deutschland 1997/98
Verlag Stadler Konstanz 1997

Bernhard Hager
100 Jahre Hauptbahnhof Wiesbaden
in: Jahrbuch für Eisenbahngeschichte 2006/07, Seite 5-25
DGEG Medien, Hövelhof 2006

Haus der Bayerischen Geschichte (Hrsg.)
Eisenbahn in Bayern 1835-2010
Augsburg 2010

Lis Künzli (Hrsg.)
Bahnhöfe. Ein literarischer Führer
Eichborn Verlag, Berlin 2007

Mihály Kubinsky
Bahnhöfe Europas- Ihre Geschichte, Kunst und Technik
Franck´sche Verlagshandlung, Stuttgart 1969

Dierk Lawrenz, Lothar Eichmann
Die Heidebahn
EK Verlag, Freiburg 1997

Peter Neumann
Berlins Bahnhöfe - gestern, heute, morgen
Jaron Verlag, Berlin 2004

Erich Preuß, Hans-Joachim Kirsche
Wunderwelt der Eisenbahn
GeraMond Verlag, München 2001

Erich Preuß
100 legendäre Bahnhöfe
Transpress, Stuttgart 2010

Ralf Roth
Das Jahrhundert der Eisenbahn
Jan Thorbecke Verlag, Ostfildern 2004

Martin Schack
Neue Bahnhöfe
Die Empfangsgebäude der Deutschen Bundesbahn 1948-1973
Verlag B. Neddermeyer, Berlin 2004

Erich Staisch
Hamburg Hauptbahnhof
Geschichte der Eisenbahn in Norddeutschland
Hoffmann und Campe, Hamburg 1981

Meinhard Sucker
Die Seilzuganlage in Hochdahl
Deutsche Bundesbahn Regionalabteilung, Düsseldorf 1988

Manfred Weltner
Bahnhöfe der Welt
GeraMond, München 2020

Malte Werning
Inselbahnen der Nordsee
Geramond, München 2003

Websites

www.de.wikipedia.org (verschiedene Wikipedia-Seiten zu
Bahnhöfen); Anekdoten u.a. zu Magdeburg Südost, Köln-
Holweide, Radebeul West (Kötzschenbroda)

www.bahn.de
Statistische Daten zu den 20 größten DB-Bahnhöfen

Bad Doberan
http://www.treffpunkt-ostsee.de/geschichten-sagen/molli-bahn-anekdote.php

Bremen St. Magnus
http://www.sankt-magnus.de/Knoop.html

Füssen
www.bahnhof-fuessen.de

Ganderkeese
http://www.hasenahlers.de/055f249c271139309/055f249c2712a1212/index.html

Gotha
www.bahnhof-gotha.de

Hemmor
http://www.niederelbebahn.de/geschichte/unterelbebahn/bahnhoefe/hemmoor/

Landsberg
www.bahnhof-landsberg.de

Neukirchen/Oberpfalz
https://www.oberpfalznetz.de/zeitung/2496999-129-wo_karl_marx_den_anschluss_verpasste-P8,1,0.html

Rolandseck
http://www.arpmuseum.org/html/haeuser/fr_bahn.html

Siemens-Fürstenbrunn
http://w3.siemens.de/siemens-stadt/anekdot0.htm

Berlin, Storkower Straße
http://www.berliner-zeitung.de/archiv/europas-laengste-fussgaengerbruecke-wird-abgerissen--
-am-montag-begannen-die-arbeiten-vom--langen-jammer--bleibt-ein-winziges-
stueck,10810590,10000972.html

Reisende und Besucher in ausgewählten Bahnhöfen in Deutschland 2017
https://www.handelsdaten.de/deutschsprachiger-einzelhandel/travel-retail-
taegliche-anzahl-besucher-reisenden-bahnhoefe

Bahnhof Regensburg
http://www.rswe.de/index_html_files/Fluegelrad%20Sonderausgabe%201%20%2
02018.pdf

Döppersberg und die Bronzelöwen
https://www.wz.de/nrw/wuppertal/historisches-foto-erinnert-an-bronzeloewen-
vom-doeppersberg_aid-35604771

Other railway station books of the author (Siehe www.bod.de)

The destiny station beyond the mountains
Short stories about 111 railway stations in the Alpine countries
Books on Demand, Norderstedt 2020

The cathedral of the winged wheel and the sugarbeet station
Trivia and Anecdotes on 222 Railway Stations in Europe.
Books on Demand, Norderstedt 2020

Grand Central Terminal and the station at the end of the world
Short stories about 222 train stations of the Americas
Books on Demand, Norderstedt 2020

The Gingerbread station at the other end of the World
Short stories about 222 train stations in Africa, Asia and Oceania
Books on Demand, Norderstedt 2020

Antwerpen CS